Cooking With Spirits

By Beverly Barbour
Drawings by David Yeadon

101 Productions
San Francisco
1976

Published by 101 Productions
834 Mission Street
San Francisco, California 94103

Distributed to the book trade in the United States by
Charles Scribner's Sons, New York, and in Canada by
Van Nostrand Reinhold Ltd., Toronto

Library of Congress Cataloging in Publication Data

Barbour, Beverly, 1927–
  Cooking with spirits.

  Includes indexes.
  1. Cookery (Liquors)   I. Title.
TX726.B33   641.6'2   76-6838
ISBN 0-912238-83-6
ISBN 0-912238-82-8 pbk.

Contents

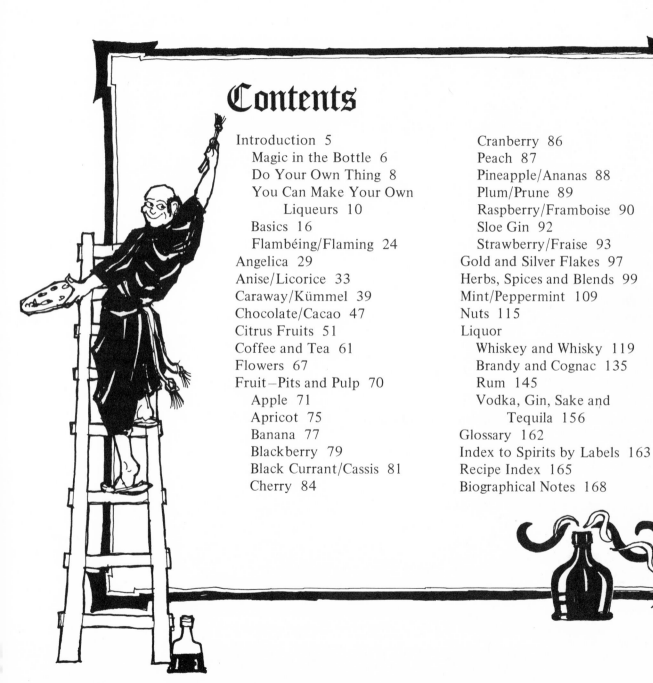

Introduction

AS ANYONE who enjoys playing the pot and pan game knows—it's the final flavor that counts. And achieving that final good taste is a matter of blending together ingredients which will complement each other, each bringing out the character of the others. Every ingredient makes a contribution, either in taste or in texture, to the final dish.

We've grown accustomed to cooking with spices and herbs, and think nothing now of sharing our wine with a thirsty recipe, but most people overlook the marvelous flavors stored in spirit bottles. Almost all spirit flavors are blends—herbs with other herbs, herbs with fruit, fruits with pits, pits with peels, peels with chocolate, chocolate with coffee, coffee with whiskey, and on and on. The variations are endless and the carefully prepared blends found in bottles can add another dimension to your cooking.

Cooking with spirits is not extravagant. It should—actually it must—be done gently, with a light touch. The spirit should bring out the natural flavor of food, not overwhelm it. Often a spoonful, or even a few drops, will lift a dish into the gourmet class. Many liqueurs are available in miniatures which hold about three tablespoons: enough for most recipes, with leftovers for the cook. You really don't have to invest in a fifth unless it's a spirit that you enjoy drinking as much as you like cooking with it.

Then, too, many flavors are available at 42° proof, which makes them half the price of higher proofs. The percentage of alcohol is lower, the flavor is still there, and they work just as well for everything except flambéing. But there are ways to save money when flambéing, too. See Flambéing/Flaming.

Then, too, should the spirit move you, You Can Make Your Own Liqueurs (see the chapter by that name). There you go, adding yet another creative dimension to cooking.

Magic in the Bottle

Liqueurs Have an Interesting and Not So Ancient History

THE FIRST MAN reported to flavor alcohol with herbs and aromatic plants was Hippocrates in the fifth century B.C. History attests to the potency of his brew; it is described as "fit only for the strongest of men."

Later, when the alchemists were hard at work in their search for eternal life (and the gold to enjoy it), the good fathers in the monasteries began to experiment with the addition of medicinal herbs to alcohol as a means of treating the illnesses within their flocks. Early records affirm that the Carmaldolite monks of the Order of St. Romulad started using Brandy mixed with the juice of very ripe plums as a remedy against malaria, around 1010 A.D.

From these monastic beginnings evolved digestifs—aids to digestion and well-being. A few of the early formulas are still being produced. Goldwasser combines two medical beliefs of the Middle Ages: that gold prevented disease and that caraway was the best remedy for stomach ailments. Benedictine is no longer produced by the Benedictine monks, but their 460-year-old recipe is still followed. Chartreuse, on the other hand, is still associated with the religious order that perfected its blend of more than 130 herbs and other flavoring agents. There are other ancient-formula digestifs which are now marketed as liqueurs.

Queen Isabella of Spain indirectly did the most to make the harsh fermented beverages of yesteryear palatable. The second voyage of Columbus brought sugarcane cuttings to the Caribbean. Within 30 years cane sugar became the leading export (after gold) from the New World to the Old. It was this sugar which served to smooth the rough edges of liquors and turn them into liqueurs.

Italy was the liqueur production center of Europe in the Middle Ages. So fond of the myriad flavors was Caterina de Medici that when she left Florence around 1532 to become the bride of the Duke of Orléans (later King Henry II of France), she included liqueur-makers in her entourage to teach her French subjects the noble art. The clever French learned well; today they lead the world in liqueur exports with 80 percent of the total world volume.

From the beginning, the famous distilleries of France were located where the fruits were grown, and to a large extent they still are. But not all liqueurs are flavored with herbs or with fruit. Other flavoring agents used include: *barks and woods* such as angostura, cinnamon, myrrh, sassafras; *roots* such as angelica, celery, ginger, orris, rhubarb, turmeric; *flowers* such as citrus blossoms, lavender, lily, poplar buds, rose, saffron; *seeds and fruits* such as aniseed, apricot stones, bitter almonds, cactus, cardamom, citrus peel, cocoa, coffee, hazel nuts, juniper berries, nutmeg, peach pits, vanilla and all edible fruits. *Honey* is a miscellaneous flavoring material whose taste depends upon which flowers the bees have been bumbling about.

Few liqueurs or fruit Brandies spend much time in a wooden cask. Brandy made from grapes is usually aged, while the other fruit Brandies are bottled immediately as the flavors are delicate and don't benefit from aging in wood. Once opened, the fruit essences will deteriorate—even in the glass the flavor goes wafting off.

Now isn't that a good rationale for pinching an inch here and there to cook with?

Do Your Own Thing

How to Cook with Liqueurs and Other Spirits

BECAUSE MOST spirits are blends, you will often have to follow the advice of your nose and tongue when cooking with them. Sniff a bit. Does the spirit smell as though it might be good in apple pie, or with lamb chops, or in whipped cream? Taste just a drop, then taste again, remembering that the alcohol will cook away and only the savor will remain.

Begin with moderation until you discover just how pervasive the flavor of a given spirit is in the finished product. The goal is not to taste the liquor distinctively, but to have the flavor blend with other ingredients, making its contribution discreetly.

Always make a written note of how much spirit you add to the recipe. If it is more than a few drops, you will need to deduct that amount from other liquids the recipe calls for. Then, too, you may find that you want just a bit more, or a bit less, of the elusive flavor next time. Or, another time you may want to experiment with an entirely different spirit.

It really is a lot of fun. But best of all are the ooh's and aah's and compliments that come from that slightly heightened, hard-to-pinpoint difference in taste.

The recipes in this book are arranged according to basic flavors, with suggestions for substitutions when any of several flavors could be used. If you have a bottle of orange-flavored liqueur, such as Cointreau, Triple-Sec or Grand Marnier on hand, look in the chapter entitled Citrus Fruits for recipes tailored to that liqueur. When a bottle of Crème de Cacao is available, check Chocolate/Cacao for inspiration.

When you're not certain what the principle flavoring agent is in any liqueur, check the Index of Spirits by Labels, which lists products by brand name. The index will help you find recipes using that spirit or a similar one. The Recipe Index lists all the recipes in the book by name as well as cross-references by type of recipe (soup, salad, dessert, etc.) and basic ingredient (chicken, pork, etc.).

You Can Make Your Own Liqueurs

... And Save Half to Two-Thirds of the Cost!

LIQUEUR MAKERS contrive their wares in any way they think will please the public, but basically liqueurs have one thing in common: They are alcohol sweetened and flavored with anything which the maker feels will create a pleasant taste. Through the years liqueur makers have come up with some extremely pleasing flavor combinations. Many of these are very complex, closely guarded secrets, and many are combinations of plant materials found only in specific areas. Nevertheless, there is nothing to stop you from making your own, either with flavoring materials you have at hand or with essences you can purchase for that purpose. You do as they do and tint one blue and another red, flavor one with cherries from your own tree and another with peppermint from the shelf. They blend and brew and so can you. Think of all the fun they've had since Hippocrates started it all.

To do it yourself you need:

AN ALCOHOL BASE: As the flavor you choose will cover most of the flavor of the alcohol used as the foundation for your liqueur, save money and buy very inexpensive charcoal-filtered Vodka (by the gallon for greatest saving) or grain neutral spirits which can then be diluted half-and-half with distilled or de-ionized water.

10

You Can Make Your Own Liqueurs

When the Christmas spirit has melted away and you're left with some bottles which you don't particularly care to drink you can use them in making liqueurs. It might be helpful to know:

Brandy blends well with most fruit and herb flavors. When you want a hint of Brandy in the flavor, buy a domestic brand. There's no need to waste money using a fine Cognac or imported Brandy.

Rum goes especially well with citrus flavors and with berries, though it is good with all fruits. The lighter Rums are best for making liqueurs, as they have less taste of their own.

Gin has limited use. Mint is about the only flavor that is pervasive enough to cover the distinctive taste of the juniper berry.

Whiskies, with the possible exception of very light Canadian Whiskies, have a distinctive taste that comes through most flavoring agents. They are best used by making sweetened versions of them as the Irish have done in making Irish Mist from Irish Whiskey.

SWEETENING: Because dry sugar does not dissolve readily in alcohol, a simple syrup should be used for sweetening. One cup of sugar boiled with one-half cup of water (just long enough to be certain all of the sugar is in solution) will sweeten three cups (a "fifth") of alcohol to produce a medium-sweet liqueur. If water is chlorinated, boil for a few minutes to drive off the chemical. Distilled water is ideal as it is completely tasteless. For a sweet crème-type liqueur use two cups of the syrup per three cups of alcohol.

You can vary the flavor by using honey (light colored, mild flavored) in place of the sugar solution and by using light brown sugar or raw sugar in the syrup. Honey makes liqueurs somewhat cloudy, but if you have the patience to let them sit undisturbed for a month you can siphon off the clear portion for sipping and leave the cloudy bottom for the cook to experiment with in the kitchen.

FLAVORINGS: The ingredients called for in the liqueur recipes given in this book are readily available. Then, too, Italian bakeshops are an excellent source of imported vials of flavorings which make excellent liqueurs. There are companies making flavoring extracts designed specifically for use in home liqueur making and these products are often available in stores which stock supplies for making wines and beers at home. If you can't secure liqueur flavorings in your area, try one of the following firms:

Wine Supply West, Inc.	The Purple Foot	Wine Maker's Haven
4324 Geary Street	3171 South 92nd Street	105 North York Road
San Francisco, CA 94118	Milwaukee, WI 53227	Hatboro, PA 19040
Telephone: (415) 221-5137	Telephone: (414) 327-2130	Telephone: (215) OS 5-2991

GLYCERINE: Commercial liqueur makers add glycerine to make their products feel heavier in the mouth. One teaspoon per quart is recommended, but it isn't a necessary ingredient.

COLORING: Any food coloring used in cooking can color home-brewed liqueurs as well.

You Can Make Your Own Liqueurs

EQUIPMENT:
- Kitchen strainer, cheesecloth and cotton cloth for filtering.
- Wide-mouth gallon jar for steeping. The kind that restaurants buy salad dressings and pickles in works perfectly.
- Wine or liqueur bottles or mason jars for storing. Glass is preferred for storage, as it prevents the liqueur's picking up "off" flavors.
- Corks or screw-on lids. Never use plastic, not even a plastic-lined lid, as the flavor of plastic transfers almost immediately to liqueurs.

GENERAL GUIDELINES FOR MAKING YOUR OWN LIQUEURS:

The flavoring material usually steeps in the alcohol base for a week or longer before it is strained and sweetened. Use a glass container and cover while steeping to prevent the loss of alcohol. After the flavoring has steeped in the alcohol for the prescribed period of time, run the liquid through an ordinary kitchen strainer to remove the large pieces of whatever flavoring material was used (plums, stick cinnamon, etc.). Then pour the liquid through cheesecloth and then through a more tightly woven cotton such as worn sheeting or a pillowcase.

When making fruit liqueurs, don't be afraid to squeeze the fruit held in the cotton to get all of the fruit flavor and the alcohol out of the pulp. Make a fourth and fifth pour through three layers of tightly woven cotton. The result should be a nice, clear liquid.

Then add the cooled sweetening syrup and blend well. To prevent any further loss of the flavoring essences to the air, bottle immediately in clean wine or liqueur bottles or in mason jars. Whatever containers you use for making and storing the liqueur should be cleaned out well with a mixture of baking soda and water to eliminate odors and tastes from the previous tenants. It is a good idea to sterilize the jars by boiling for 15 minutes, or to run them through the dishwasher without any detergent or soap to leave an unwanted flavor.

Cap bottles tightly to prevent loss of alcohol and flavor. Corks permit some evaporation unless sealed with foil or wax. A screw-on lid of some sort is the most efficient closure. The liqueur should then be stored at least two weeks before using.

ALMOND-CHERRY LIQUEUR
Somewhat like Cherry Heering

3 cups pitted Bing cherries
1 cup cherry pits
3 cups Brandy
1/2 cup sugar or other sweetening
1/4 cup water

Tie cherry pits together in a cloth and smash with a hammer. Place pits, cherries and Brandy in a covered jar and let stand 3 weeks. Strain well and squeeze cherries to remove all juice. Combine sugar and water and boil until sugar is completely dissolved. Cool and add to filtered Brandy mixture. Pour into glass container, cover tightly and let stand about 2 weeks before serving.
Makes about 2 pints

ANGELICA LIQUEUR
Use where Galliano, Strega or yellow Chartreuse would be suitable

3 cups Vodka or other spirit
1 tablespoon chopped angelica root
1 stick cinnamon
1 whole clove
1/8 teaspoon ground nutmeg
1/8 teaspoon ground mace
2 cups sugar or other sweetening
1 cup water

Combine all ingredients except sugar and water in a large jar and let steep for 1 week or longer. Combine sugar and water and boil until sugar is completely dissolved. Cool. Filter Vodka mixture and add cooled syrup. Pour into glass container, cover tightly and let stand about 2 weeks before serving.
Makes about 2 pints

13

You Can Make Your Own Liqueurs

CARAWAY LIQUEUR
Use as you would Kümmel

2 tablespoons crushed caraway seed
1 tablespoon crushed fennel seed
1-1/2 teaspoons ground cumin
3 cups Vodka or other spirit
2 cups sugar or other sweetening
1 cup water

Steep the flavorings in the alcohol for 10 days in a tightly covered container. Combine sugar and water and boil until sugar is completely dissolved. Cool. Filter Vodka mixture and add cooled syrup. Pour into glass container, cover tightly and let stand about 2 weeks before serving.
Makes about 2 pints

COFFEE LIQUEUR
Made with Vodka it resembles Kahlúa; use Rum and it is more like Tia Maria

4 cups sugar or other sweetening
2 cups water
2 inches vanilla bean
6 tablespoons freeze-dried coffee, or
3 tablespoons instant coffee
3 cups Vodka or light Rum
2 teaspoons glycerine (optional)

Boil sugar, 1-1/2 cups water and vanilla bean broken in several places for 30 minutes. Dissolve freeze-dried or instant coffee in 1/2 cup boiling water. Shake together the sugar syrup and the coffee solution. Add alcohol and glycerine; let stand 2 weeks in covered jar. Remove vanilla bean. Store in tightly covered glass container.
Makes about 2-1/2 pints

LICORICE LIQUEUR
Use as you would Anisette or Pernod

2 tablespoons crushed star anise
3 cups Vodka or other spirit
3 cups sugar or other sweetening
1-1/2 cups water

Let anise steep in alcohol for 10 days in a tightly covered container. Combine sugar and water and boil until sugar is completely dissolved. Cool. Filter Vodka mixture and add cooled syrup. Pour into glass container, cover tightly and let stand about 2 weeks before serving.
Makes about 2-1/2 pints

MINT LIQUEUR
Use as you would Crème de Menthe

4 cups sugar or other sweetening
2 cups water
3 cups Vodka or other spirit
1 teaspoon glycerine (optional)
2 to 3 teaspoons peppermint extract

Boil sugar and water together to make a syrup. Cool. Shake together with remaining ingredients, adding peppermint extract to taste. Pour into glass container, cover tightly and let stand about 2 weeks before serving.
Makes about 3 pints

ORANGE LIQUEUR
Use as you would Cointreau, Triple-Sec, Grand Marnier, etc.

3 oranges
3 cups Brandy, or Brandy and Vodka
1 cup honey (orange blossom preferred)

Peel oranges using only the outer orange-colored portion of the skin and removing all of the bitter white inner peel. Reserve pulp for other use. Place orange peel in a large jar with the alcohol. Cover and steep for 3 weeks. Remove peel, add honey and let stand 3 or 4 days. Strain off clear portion for drinking; the cloudy remainder is excellent for cooking. Store in tightly covered glass container.
Makes about 2 pints

RASPBERRY LIQUEUR
Use as you would Crème de Framboise

1-1/2 cups raspberries (fresh preferred)
3 cups Brandy or other spirit
1 cup water
2 cups sugar

Cover raspberries with Brandy and shake together well. Let steep for 7 days in a covered jar. Squeeze fruit to extract all of the juice and alcohol. Filter. Boil water and sugar together until sugar is completely dissolved; cool. Combine filtered alcohol and cooled syrup. Pour into glass container, cover tightly and let stand about 2 weeks before serving.
Makes about 2-1/2 pints

Basics

Sauces, Pastries, Etc.

SEASONING SALT

Recipes calling for seasoning salt in this book have been tested using Lawry's brand seasoning salt. Each cook may use the commercial product of his or her choice in these recipes, or may substitute a homemade herb salt if desired. Use any seasoning salt sparingly, tasting as you go.

CUMBERLAND SAUCE

This sauce enhances any pâté or terrine and is marvelous, too, with cold venison and most lamb dishes

1 teaspoon chopped shallot
1 tablespoon orange peel, cut in very fine
   julienne strips
1 tablespoon lemon peel, cut in very fine
   julienne strips
1 cup red currant jelly, melted
1 teaspoon or more Dijon mustard
1 cup Port
juice of 1 orange
juice of 1 lemon
salt
ground ginger
cayenne

Tie shallot and peels together in cheesecloth and simmer in water to cover 2 minutes; drain and combine with remaining ingredients. Adjust seasonings to taste. Serve immediately.
Makes about 2-1/2 cups

HOLLANDAISE SAUCE
An easy-to-make recipe for the classic sauce

4 egg yolks
1/4 pound butter, cut in thirds
2 to 3 teaspoons lemon juice
salt
white pepper
nutmeg

Place egg yolks and 1/3 of the butter in top of double boiler. (Water in bottom of double boiler should not touch top pan.) Cook over *hot, not boiling,* water until butter melts, stirring rapidly. Add 1/3 more of the butter and continue stirring. As mixture thickens and butter melts, add remaining butter, stirring constantly. When all of butter is melted, remove pan from hot water; stir rapidly 2 minutes longer. Stir in lemon juice a teaspoon at a time; season with a dash of salt, a dash of white pepper and a few grains of nutmeg. Heat again over hot water and stir constantly until thickened, 2 to 3 minutes. Remove from heat at once. If sauce curdles, immediately beat in 1 or 2 tablespoons boiling water.
Makes 1 cup

BLENDER HOLLANDAISE
Made with orange juice, it's a version of Maltaise Sauce

3 egg yolks
1 to 2 tablespoons lemon or orange juice
dash cayenne or nutmeg
1/4 pound butter
few drops dry Vermouth

Place egg yolks, lemon juice and cayenne or nutmeg in blender container. Cover; quickly turn blender on and off. In a small pan heat butter until melted and almost boiling. Turn blender on high speed; slowly pour in butter, blending until thick and fluffy, about 30 seconds. Hold over warm, not hot, water until ready to serve.
Makes 1 cup

Note: If using orange juice you may wish to add a small amount of orange-flavored liqueur.

Basics

BASIC CRÊPE BATTER

1 cup half-and-half
1 cup water*
4 eggs
1 teaspoon salt
2 cups all-purpose flour, sifted
3-1/2 tablespoons melted butter

Place all ingredients except butter in a blender. Blend at highest speed, covered, for 1-1/2 minutes. Scrape flour sticking to the sides down into batter. Add the melted butter, cover and blend for another 1/2 minute. It is important that this batter rest (right in the blender jar) in the refrigerator for 3 hours before using. This gives the flour time to expand in the liquids, a process that provides light and tender crêpes.

The batter must be of the consistency of medium cream and should coat a spoon. If too heavy, it not only makes thick crêpes but spreads too slowly in the pan and lumps in the center. If necessary the batter can be thinned by stirring in small amounts of milk.

To be a true crêpe, a pancake must be parchment-thin, no more than 1/16 inch thick. Thus you must be careful about the amount of batter you pour into the pan. Use 1-1/2 tablespoons for a 5-inch crêpe (or use a spouted glass jigger marked in ounces and pour in just under 1 ounce for a 5-inch crêpe and just over 1 ounce for a 6-inch crêpe). A small ladle is handy, but with the cooking of a few crêpes you'll work out the precise amount of batter without any problem.

Brush pan lightly with oil. Place it over high heat, testing it with a drop of cold water. When that instantly evaporates, it's ready. Reduce heat to medium. Place blender jar with batter in a convenient place with a long spoon beside it to stir the batter frequently. Remove pan from heat and immediately pour the measured batter into the pan, quickly tipping pan from side to side to completely cover the bottom with a thin coating of batter. If there is excess batter, pour it back into the blender. Place pan over medium heat (if holes appear in crêpe, spoon on small amounts of batter just to cover) and when the crêpe begins to look dry, is bubbling from the center and appears firm, slip a spatula under the edge and flip it over. The entire cooking operation averages a total of 1 minute for both sides, more for the first side than for the second. After you've made a few crêpes, you'll get the timing.

The first crêpe is a test. Discard it. You'll note that the side cooked first will be golden brown, more attractive than the spotty second side. That's as it should be. The second side is the inside—the portion that is filled and doesn't show. Stack the cooked crêpes; this keeps them moist and in shape. They may also be separated with waxed paper, wrapped in a cloth and frozen.
Makes 30 5-inch crêpes

*This recipe can be varied with other liquids such as clam juice, apple juice or a liqueur to give the crêpe a special flavor to match or complement the filling you will use.

BASIC PASTRY
*This never-fail crust is easy to handle
and can be rerolled without toughening*

3 cups sifted all-purpose flour
1 teaspoon salt
1 teaspoon baking powder
1-1/4 cups shortening
1 egg, well beaten
5 tablespoons water
1 tablespoon cider or white vinegar

Sift flour, salt and baking powder together into a bowl; add shortening and cut into flour mixture until it resembles coarse cornmeal. Beat together egg, water and vinegar and add to flour mixture all at once. Stir with a fork until flour is just moistened. Divide dough and roll out on lightly floured surface.
Makes 2 double crusts or 4 single crusts

Note: Unused dough can be wrapped in plastic and stored in the refrigerator 2 weeks or longer; dough freezes well.

PASTRY FOR TART SHELLS
*A tender crust that doesn't need
to be rolled and cut*

6 tablespoons butter
4-1/2 tablespoons granulated sugar
1 whole egg, or 1 egg yolk plus 1 tablespoon
   cold water
1-1/2 cups sifted all-purpose flour
1 teaspoon baking powder
1/4 teaspoon salt
confectioners' sugar

Preheat oven to 350°. Cream butter and sugar together; beat in egg. Sift flour, baking powder and salt together and work into the creamed mixture. Dip fingers in flour and press dough to line small or regular-size muffin pans or tart shells. Fill the unbaked pastry with mince or filling of choice and bake 30 minutes. Remove from oven and dust with confectioners' sugar while still hot.
Makes 32 small tarts; about 20 larger

Basics

VOL-AU-VENT
The secret is to have butter
and dough the same consistency

A vol-au-vent looks more difficult to make than it actually proves to be. There are three essential ingredients: a cool kitchen, time to let the dough relax and chill between rollings, and a recipe which will produce a strong yet tender puff paste.

There must be as many basic formulas and differing methods for puff pastry as there are French cookbooks and perhaps it is best for the amateur vol-au-vent maker to begin with a "rough" or "half-puff" pastry—actually a cross between a pie crust and a true puff paste. The recipe makes a sturdy, easy-to-handle dough that endures the rough treatment sometimes necessary in shaping your first vol-au-vent.

Once you've played the making and shaping game, you may want to move on to the second puff paste recipe in which the butter is separate from the layers of dough. The French call it *pâté feuilletée.* Reducing the layers to the thinness of leaves requires much rolling, molding and rerolling but the result is worth it. Good puff paste will triple in thickness when it bakes.

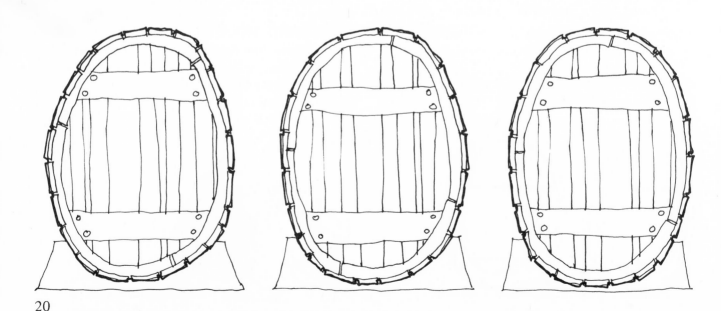

ROUGH OR HALF-PUFF PASTE
Fast and easy, it produces a sturdy crust

Paste:
4 cups sifted all-purpose flour
3/4 cup butter*
3/4 cup lard
1 teaspoon vinegar
3/4 cup ice water

Glaze:
1 egg
1 tablespoon cold water

*If using unsalted butter, add 1 teaspoon salt; sift with flour into mixing bowl and proceed as directed.

Sift the flour into a large mixing bowl. Slice the sticks of butter and lard into the flour, in pieces about 1/4 inch thick. Gently stir so that the pieces will be well coated with flour. Combine vinegar with ice water and add a little to the bowl; mix lightly, keeping the squares of fat as intact as you can. Gradually add enough of the remaining liquid to form a moderately stiff dough. On a pastry cloth or lightly floured surface roll the dough into a long rectangle and fold equally in thirds; then fold into thirds again. Again roll into a long rectangle and fold as before. Repeat this process twice more. If the dough becomes difficult to handle, chill 30 minutes between rollings.

Wrap dough in waxed paper and/or a plastic bag. Let it rest in the refrigerator a minimum of 30 minutes (1 hour is better). Preheat oven to 450°. Shape the vol-au-vent (below) and bake 10 minutes. Reduce heat to 350° and bake 20 minutes longer. After the first 20 minutes, brush with glaze made by beating egg and water together. Cool, fill and serve as directed below.
Makes a vol-au-vent which
when filled will serve 4 to 6

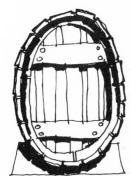
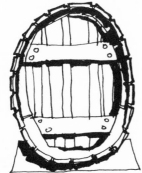

Basics

PUFF PASTRY
Flaky, tender and easy to make

Paste:
1 pound butter*
3-1/2 cups sifted all-purpose flour
1 cup plus 1 tablespoon ice water
2 teaspoons white vinegar or lemon juice

Glaze:
1 egg
1 tablespoon cold water

Cut each stick of butter into 3 lengthwise strips. Place the 12 strips on waxed paper and refrigerate until ready to use. Sift the flour into a large mixing bowl. Combine ice water with vinegar or lemon juice and gradually add the liquid to the flour, stirring and tossing with a fork to form a dry dough. Knead the dough on a *very* lightly floured surface 10 minutes, then cover with plastic and let rest 30 minutes.

On a pastry cloth or lightly floured surface roll the dough as thinly as you can into the shape of a rectangle. Arrange half of the chilled butter strips horizontally on the center third of the dough in 2 rows, leaving a 1/2-inch margin of dough at the narrow ends. Fold one of the remaining thirds of the dough over the butter and seal the 3 open edges with the heel of the hand. Place the remaining 6 strips of butter on top, leaving a 1/2-inch margin at the edges. Fold the remaining third of the dough over the butter and seal the open edges with the heel of the hand.

Tap the dough lightly with a rolling pin to flatten the butter. Gently roll out lengthwise into a rectangle about 1/4 inch thick, or as thinly as you can without breaking the pastry. Fold the rectangle into thirds, and then into thirds again. Roll out again as thinly as you can without breaking the dough. Refold. At this point the butter will have become quite soft and it is best to wrap the dough in waxed paper and/or plastic and chill 30 minutes. Roll once more and then wrap dough and leave until ready to shape the vol-au-vent.

After shaping (below), bake the vol-au-vent in a preheated 400° oven 15 minutes, then turn oven to 350° and continue baking 30 minutes longer. Beat egg and water together to make a glaze; brush surface of vol-au-vent with glaze 10 to 15 minutes before removing from oven. Cool, fill and serve as directed below.
Makes a vol-au-vent which
when filled will serve 4 to 6

*If using unsalted butter, add 1 teaspoon salt; sift with flour into mixing bowl and proceed as directed.

SHAPING

Bottom A pastry cloth makes the rolling of puff paste a much simpler task, but lacking one, any lightly floured surface will do. Roll the dough into a long rectangle. It will be too long for the pastry cloth, so concentrate on one end of the rectangle, rolling it 1/8 inch thick and wide enough to cut a 9- or 10-inch circle. Use a cake pan, plate or pan lid as a cutting guide, saving all of the trimmings for later use. Place the cut circle on a slightly dampened baking sheet (the moisture gives the pastry something to cling to); don't use Teflon. Prick the circle here and there with a fork to permit it to rise uniformly in the oven. (Later you might want to experiment with an egg shape or a rectangular loaf shape.)

Sphere for Shaping Make a ball by filling about 15 square inches of foil, parchment or tissue paper with crumbled strips of parchment or tissue paper. The finished sphere should be 5 to 6 inches in diameter. Place the ball in the center of the circle of dough and brush the perimeter of the circle with cold water.

Cover Roll the other end of the rectangle into a 13-inch circle, 1/8 inch thick, and fit the dough over the ball, being careful not to tear the pastry. The top circle should be large enough to cover the dampened perimeter of the bottom circle. Trim any dough which extends beyond edge of bottom circle. The top and bottom circles must have enough pastry to form a good tight seal all around. If the base is sufficiently large, bring the bottom up around the edge of the top crust and seal the 3 layers of pastry together. If not, press the 2 layers together, crimping as you would to form the seal on the edge of a pie.

Roll the remaining dough 1/8 inch thick and cut a 4-inch circle. Moisten one side and center it on top of the dome, damp side down, to form a cap. Prick the pastry in several places with a larding needle, a fine knitting needle or a two-tined fork to allow the steam to escape from inside.

Scraps Don't throw away any of the paste from shaping the vol-au-vent. The bits and pieces can be cut into fanciful shapes and used to trim the vol-au-vent. Adhere them with water as you did the lid. Piercing through both the add-on and the dome will also help hold the pieces in place during the puffing and growing process of baking.

AFTER BAKING

Remove from baking sheet to a rack to cool. When cool enough to handle, cut around the edge of the smaller circle used to cap the dome with a sharp-pointed knife. Carefully lift off the 4-inch circle and set aside. When the vol-au-vent is cool cut through the foil or paper and pull out the shredded paper a few pieces at a time. Then gently remove empty foil ball.

If desired the unfilled shell can be reheated before filling, but the heat from the hot sauce inside will warm it sufficiently at serving time. Fill it and cover with its little cap. Serve by cutting the vol-au-vent with a sharp knife and spooning the sauce over.

𝕱lambéing/𝕱laming

"It Impresses the Guests and Doesn't Seem to Hurt the Food"
—Ernie Byfield, **The Pump Room**

FIRE AND WATER are reputed to be the two greatest attractions to man. (I don't know where that leaves legs and cleavage in the scheme of things.) But, 'tis true—when there are flames dancing, it's difficult to look at anything else, and flaming food is a source of wonder and delight.

The secret of flambéing foods is to use a high-proof alcohol and to heat the sugar. It is the alcohol that supplies the flame and the higher proof the alcohol, the easier the dish will be to ignite and the higher and longer lasting the flame will be. High-proof Brandy and Rum are most often used in flambéing. Approximately 100° proof is needed for ignition at room temperature; at 80° proof the spirit must be heated to 160° before it will ignite.

As the burned-off spirit does leave flavor behind, the burning agent used should be chosen for its taste contribution to the dish. If this weren't true you would simply flambé using clear alcohol. You can mix tasteless grain neutral spirits with a good-tasting liqueur to increase the flame and its longevity.

Another alternative, and a less expensive one, is to use one of the products currently found in gourmet shops that used to be available only through suppliers to the restaurant industry. Flambé Fanfare is an example. It's 175° proof and comes in five flavors: Brandy, Rum, Orange, Curaçao (a more bitter orange character than the regular orange) and Herb (quite like the angelica-flavored liqueurs, Galliano and Strega). The products aren't taxed as alcoholic beverages and can be used in cooking as well as in flambéing. When flambéing with them, or with any other high-proof alcohol, *never* pour the liquid directly from the bottle into the flame, as the fire may follow the alcohol right up to the bottle, your elbow and your eyebrows. It sometimes even goes into the bottle causing a ball of fire to shoot out, cannon fashion. That can really warm up a party, but not happily!

As warm alcohol will ignite much more quickly than cold, the proper procedure is to stir a bit of the spirit into the sauce used, then warm it, float more spirit on top and ignite the warmed sauce. The secret to having the alcohol float on top of the sauce is to have the sauce thick enough to keep it on top. If the spirit is diluted too much by a thin sauce or juices, it won't ignite.

So dim the lights, warm the spirit and set the food on fire. You'll dazzle your guests!

24

CHAMPAGNE SAUCE FOR TURKEY
Flambé the sauce and
launch the bird in a blaze of glory

1 cup pan drippings
1-1/2 cups half-and-half
1 cup Champagne
3 tablespoons Cognac

Remove turkey to a platter and skim excess fat from the pan drippings. Return 1 cup of drippings to pan; stir in half-and-half, scraping brown bits from the pan bottom. Warm sauce, but do not simmer. Add Champagne. The Cognac can be stirred in and warmed with the sauce or it can be warmed separately and used to flambé the sauce at serving time.
Makes 3-1/2 cups

1776 MINCE PIE OR TARTS
Carry it to the table with a blazing star

pastry for a double-crust pie, see Basics
3 tablespoons orange-flavored liqueur or Brandy
2-1/2 to 3 cups mincemeat filling, page 152
additional liqueur or Brandy

Prepare 1 recipe Basic Pastry; use 1/2 of dough to make pie or tarts and refrigerate or freeze remainder. Line an 8-inch pie pan or tart shells with pastry. Stir liqueur or Brandy into mincemeat and spread over pastry. Cover with a top crust from which you have cut a large star. Bake at 400° for 25 to 30 minutes until a light golden brown. Cool. Dredge with granulated or superfine sugar, if you wish. At serving time warm a small amount (1 to 2 tablespoons) additional liqueur or Brandy and pour into center of the star; ignite.
Serves 4 to 6

Flambéing/Flaming

FLAMING SHRIMP
An interesting appetizer, hors d'oeuvre or entrée

1/2 pound shrimp
2 tablespoons butter
salt
freshly ground pepper
dill, fresh or dill weed
1/4 cup Rum

Shell and devein shrimp, leaving tails on. Sauté in butter over medium heat until meat is pink. Add salt, pepper and dill. Warm Rum, pour over shrimp and ignite. Serve at once.
Serves 2 to 8, depending upon use

COFFEE ICE CREAM WITH FLAMING NUT SAUCE
The ice cream can be molded, or served by the scoop

1/2 gallon coffee ice cream, slightly softened
2 tablespoons butter or margarine
3/4 cup coarsely chopped Brazil nuts, pecans or macadamia nuts
1/4 cup Brandy

Pack ice cream into a fancy 2-quart metal mold, cover and return to freezer for at least 2 hours or until solidly frozen. When ready to serve, unmold onto chilled plate. Melt butter, add nuts and brown lightly. Add Brandy and warm slightly. Do not stir. Ignite warmed Brandy and pour sauce over the ice cream.
Serves 10

MERINGUE SHELL GLACÉ
A melting meringue to fill
with ice cream and whole berries

5 egg whites
1-1/4 cups granulated sugar
1 teaspoon orange-flavored liqueur
2 pints ice cream
1 pint whole strawberries, hulled
Flaming Strawberry Sauce, following

Preheat oven to 300° and butter a 10-inch pie pan
or spring-form pan. Beat egg whites until foamy.
Gradually add sugar, 1 tablespoon at a time, beating well after each addition; continue beating several minutes after all of the sugar is added, until
the egg whites are very stiff and glossy. Beat in
liqueur. Spoon meringue into buttered pan, shaping a depression in the center. Bake 45 minutes to
1 hour, until very lightly browned. Cool. (If you
wish to prepare days ahead, you can slip the cooled
meringue into a plastic bag, fasten well and store in
the freezer; thaw before serving.)
  Scoop ice cream into small balls and refreeze.
When frozen, fill meringue with ice cream balls and
whole berries. Pour on the Flaming Strawberry
Sauce and flambé at the table.
Serves 6 to 8

FLAMING STRAWBERRY SAUCE
A tart purée to flambé at the table

strawberries to make 1 cup purée (less than 1 pint)
2 tablespoons undiluted frozen orange juice
  concentrate
1 tablespoon currant jelly
2 tablespoons Brandy
3 tablespoons orange-flavored liqueur

Bring purée, juice concentrate and jelly to simmering temperature. In a separate pan combine the
Brandy and liqueur and warm slightly. Pour the
strawberry purée over the ice cream and fruit in
the Meringue Shell Glacé (or over the dessert of
your choice). Ignite the heated Brandy and liqueur
and pour the blazing spirits over all.

Angelica

Angelica

As Vanilla Is to Pastries, Angelica Is to Herb Blends

LIQUEURS flavored with angelica are good on virtually any kind of ice cream and as flavoring in cream pies, puddings, custards and mousses—even on fresh fruits, though some do not enjoy them heavily spiked with herbs this way. When your nose perceives that the contents of the bottle is herby or spicy, check the chapter on Herbs, Spices and Blends for recipes.

The angelica itself is a beautiful plant—even its name is lovely. Herb angelica or archangelica means "root of the Holy Ghost" or "herb of angels" and it is supposed to have protected those who used it from the plague. Angelica grows wild in alpine areas from Lapland to Spain and its uses are almost as varied as the areas in which it is found. It has been regarded as a stimulant, a cure for stomach troubles and an antispasmodic. In Lapland the leaves are smoked like tobacco. In England the young shoots are relished in salads. In France angelica is valued mostly for its stalk, which is candied in sugar and used by candy makers, bakers and liqueur makers. In the United States it is even used as flavoring for sweet, white wines.

The discreet flavor of angelica is hard to describe, but it has a pleasant, musk-like scent. Its flavor may be distinguished in yellow *Chartreuse,* though there are many herbs blended in that liqueur. *Angelic Liqueur (Liqueur d'Angelique)* probably has angelica in its most pure form as the stalks of the plant are macerated in Brandy, but it also contains some other plants from the Pyrénées.

Krambambuli is a German variation which includes extracts of violets. *Raspail* is a yellow French liqueur based upon angelica as well as calamus, myrrh and other exotic ingredients. Raspail was originated in 1847 by a forerunner of Pasteur named Francois Vincent Raspail, who believed his concoction to have digestive and medicinal properties. He originally called it "veritable liqueur hygiénique et de dessert." An Italian-inspired liqueur, *Tuaca,* seems to be a combination of angelica, coffee, chocolate and vanilla. *Strega* and *Galliano* are other Italian liqueurs based upon angelica and herbs. The Basques simply call their own sweet, yellow version *Angelica.*

29

Angelica

ANGELICA ALMOND CAKE
A delicate beauty with subtle flavor

3 eggs
1-1/2 cups granulated sugar
1 teaspoon Crème de Noyau or Crème de Almond
1-3/4 cups sifted cake flour
1-1/2 teaspoons baking powder
1/4 teaspoon salt
3/4 cup milk, scalded
3 tablespoons Galliano or other angelica-
    flavored liqueur (not yellow Chartreuse)
Sour Cream Filling, following
1 large or 2 small bananas, sliced
1 cup heavy cream, whipped
1/4 cup toasted almonds

Preheat oven to 350°. Line 2 round 9-inch layer pans with waxed paper; butter the paper. Beat eggs and sugar together until light and fluffy. Add liqueur. Sift dry ingredients together and fold into egg mixture alternately with hot milk until blended. Pour into prepared pans. Bake 25 to 30 minutes. Cool 5 minutes in pans on rack. Turn out of pans onto rack and remove waxed paper. Cool.

Sprinkle each cooled layer with Galliano. Spread the bottom layer with Sour Cream Filling and cover with sliced bananas; top with second layer. Spread top with whipped cream and decorate with toasted almonds.
Serves 8 or more

SOUR CREAM FILLING
Delicious in any cake, including chocolate

1/2 cup granulated sugar
2 eggs
1/2 cup sour cream
1-1/2 tablespoons butter
1/4 cup toasted almonds, chopped

Combine sugar, eggs, sour cream and butter in the top of a double boiler. Cook until thick, stirring often. Cool, then mix in nuts.

SURPRISING STEAMED PUDDING
Yellow Chartreuse, Angelica, Galliano or one of their relatives may be used

2 teaspoons baking soda
2 cups ground or grated raw potatoes
2 cups ground or grated raw carrots
2 cups ground suet
2 cups golden raisins
2 cups packed brown sugar
2 eggs
3 tablespoons yellow Chartreuse
3 cups all-purpose flour
1 teaspoon ground cinnamon
1 teaspoon salt
1/2 teaspoon ground cloves
1/2 teaspoon ground nutmeg
Prohibition Sauce, following
Whipped Cream Custard, following

Sprinkle soda over the potatoes and combine with remaining ingredients in the order listed. The batter should be moist but not wet. Pack into well-greased and floured 2-quart mold, filling about 3/4 full. Cover and steam for 2-1/2 hours; test for doneness as you would a cake. Remove cover and cool for 10 minutes. Remove from mold and top each portion of pudding with Prohibition Sauce and then a dollop of Whipped Cream Custard.
Serves 8 to 12

Note: Pudding can be made ahead and stored, either in the cupboard or, better, the refrigerator. It will keep forever in the freezer. Before serving slip into greased mold, cover and steam for an hour to heat through. (May take longer if frozen.)

PROHIBITION SAUCE
Bourbon or any angelica- or almond-based liqueur will do

1/2 cup butter or margarine
1 cup granulated sugar
2 eggs
2/3 cup water
1 teaspoon grated lemon rind
liqueur of choice to taste

In the top of a double boiler cream butter and sugar together; beat in eggs. Add water and grated rind. Just before serving, heat the sauce in a double boiler, stirring with a whisk until it thickens. Stir in liqueur.
Makes 1-1/4 cups

WHIPPED CREAM CUSTARD
An angelica- or orange-flavored liqueur can be used

2 cups sifted confectioners' sugar
1 cup milk
6 tablespoons butter or margarine
4 egg yolks, beaten
2 teaspoons vanilla extract
1 teaspoon liqueur, or to taste
1/2 cup heavy cream, whipped

Combine sugar and milk in a saucepan over medium heat. Add butter and stir until melted. Stir 2 tablespoons of the hot mixture into egg yolks, then add yolks to the hot milk mixture, stirring until mixture thickens. Cool. Just before serving stir in vanilla and add liqueur to taste; fold into the whipped cream.
Makes 2-1/4 cups

PINEAPPLE-GALLIANO ICE CREAM
The flavors blend beautifully

3 cups grated fresh pineapple
juice of 1 lemon
2 tablespoons Galliano
1-1/2 cups granulated sugar
2 cups heavy cream
1 cup milk

Purée grated pineapple in an electric blender. Combine pulp with lemon juice, Galliano and sugar; let stand 3 hours in the refrigerator. Add cream and milk and churn-freeze.

Anise

Anise/Licorice

A Lick of Licorice Brightens Fish and Green Vegetables

ANY AND ALL of the licorice-flavored liqueurs have a surprising variety of uses in cooking. The secret is to add even less than you would when using another liqueur. A tiny, miniscule bit is enough, as you want just a hint of the licorice flavor. But the anise taste does marvelous things for such green vegetable dishes as spinach soufflé, broccoli soup, creamed spinach, green bean casseroles and cold cucumber soup. Fish soups and bouillabaisse take kindly to anise, too, as do almost all fish and seafood preparations. And any recipe with fennel as an ingredient is doubly good with a few drops of its flavor-mate.

These liqueurs are particularly popular in the countries bordering the Mediterranean. They range from very delicate, sweet types to the stronger and drier flavors. The licorice taste has two sources: the strong-scented but mild-flavored green anise which is widely grown in Italy, and Chinese star anise, with pods resembling starfish.

The Bordeaux area in France has been famous for *Anisette* almost since the monks began using it in the Middle Ages to make their cure-alls more palatable. Marie Brizard of Bordeaux, born in 1714, is said to have inherited a secret formula for the production of Anisette. (A more romantic tale has a West Indian traveler confiding the recipe to her in a moment of passion.) Whatever her source, she proved herself an enterprising businesswoman. She and her nephew made Anisette a cornerstone in the foundation of one of the leading firms in the French liqueur industry.

Amsterdam also produces an anise liqueur, called *Anisette de Hollande*. It is similar to *Anisette de Bordeaux* in that both are sweet, but dissimilar in that the Dutch Anisette tastes of bitter almonds.

Pernod is one of the most popular and best known of the licorice-flavored drinks. It is reminiscent in flavor and character of the forbidden Absinthe which was outlawed in France and Switzerland as the wormwood in its formula was thought to make men go blind and to hinder the conception of children. A gentleman named M. Pernod had popularized Absinthe and when it could no longer be legally sold he turned to making a lower-proof beverage, without wormwood, which was flavored much like Absinthe. This was, and still is, called Pernod.

Anise/Licorice

La Tintaine is yet another liqueur of licorice flavor and French origin. It used to come to market with a sprig of fennel in the bottle.

Anisetta Stellata, Elixir de China and *Anesone* are Italian anise-flavored spirits, not as sweet as Anisette. There are a number of liqueurs with some anise in their composition made near Rome: *Sambuco, Sambuca Romana, Patrician Sambuca,* etc. Witch elderbush adds a special touch of freshness to Sambuca Romana's flavor. *Absinate* is a pale green blend of Italian herbs with a subtle anise taste.

Anis Del Mono and *Ojen* are Spanish anise liqueurs. *Escarchado* is a Portuguese version of the liqueur.

Mastika comes from the Balkans. *Mastic* and *Masticha* are native to Greece and Cyprus. These are made from aniseed and the sap of trees belonging to the cashew family, one of which comes from the island of Chios. The Greek *Ouzo* is drier than the Northern European types.

Arrack, Arraki, Arack, Arak, Raki, etc. are names derived from the Arabic "juice" or "sweat" and designate "native spirits." They are rough drinks flavored with whatever herbs and spices are native to the area where they're made. Anise is often among them.

Tres Castillos is a Puerto Rican version of anisette, sweetened with sugar candy.

AVOCADO CLAM-UP
A cold soup you can make in minutes

1 ripe avocado
1 can (10-1/2 ounces) cream of chicken soup
1 can (7-1/4 to 10-1/2 ounces) minced clams
1 cup milk
1/2 cup heavy cream
1 teaspoon lemon juice
1 teaspoon Pernod or Anisette
1 teaspoon horseradish
2 dashes Tabasco
salt

Combine avocado meat, undiluted chicken soup, clams with their juice and milk. Blend in electric blender in 2 batches until smooth. Blend in remaining ingredients, seasoning to taste. Add green food coloring if you feel the soup is too pale. Chill. The soup thickens as it stands. If you prefer it thinner or have need to stretch it, add additional milk and cream.

Serve sprinkled with grated lemon peel or with salted whipped cream and grated peel.
Serves 6 to 8

PERNOD PEAS IN SOUR CREAM
*A cool, refreshing, good-traveling
vegetable-cum-salad*

1-1/2 pounds shelled peas, fresh or frozen
   (about 4 cups)
1 cup sour cream
1 teaspoon horseradish
1/2 teaspoon salt
1/4 teaspoon dry mint or
   1 teaspoon chopped fresh mint
1/2 teaspoon Pernod
3 scallions, thinly sliced (including green tops)
1 red apple, unpeeled, cored and finely chopped

If fresh peas are used, cook them until barely tender and then cool. If frozen peas are used, turn them onto paper towels to thaw.
   Combine remaining ingredients. Combine with thawed peas. Chill.
Serves 8 to 10

BRANDIED CHICKEN WITH ANISETTE
A delicately aromatic dish that is quickly prepared

4 chicken breasts or 1 whole chicken, skinned
3 tablespoons butter
1 clove garlic, minced
1 small onion, finely chopped
1 cup sliced mushrooms (optional)
salt
white pepper
1 cube chicken bouillon, crushed
1/3 cup water
1/3 cup Brandy
1 teaspoon Anisette or other anise-flavored liqueur

If using whole chicken, cut into serving portions. Slowly brown pieces or breasts in butter. Add garlic, onion and mushrooms; cook until onion is transparent. Season with salt and pepper. Pour off any fat. Add crushed bouillon cube, water, Brandy and Anisette. Cover and cook over low heat or in a 325° oven for about 30 minutes.
Serves 4

ANISETTE OR PERNOD BUTTER
Try this with seafood or green vegetables;
melt and serve with lobster or crab

1/2 pound salted butter, softened
4 teaspoons Anisette or Pernod
1 teaspoon chervil
finely chopped parsley (optional)

Cut butter into mixing bowl; beat in liqueur and chervil. Pack into individual pots or shape into 2 logs and roll in parsley. Store in refrigerator or freezer.
Makes 1/2 pound

Pernod, or any anise-flavored liqueur, does good things for spinach.

Flavor sweetened water with an anise-flavored liqueur and freeze for a refreshing sorbet.

SCALLOPS, MUSSELS OR SHRIMP WITH AVOCADO
An elegant and easy lunch or breakfast dish

2 tablespoons butter
2 tablespoons all-purpose flour
3/4 cup milk
1/2 teaspoon salt
freshly ground pepper
1 egg yolk
1/4 cup dry white wine
1 teaspoon lemon juice
1 cup raw or precooked shellfish (about 1/4 pound)
1 hard-cooked egg, chopped
few drops Pernod
1 avocado, sliced
crêpes (see Basics), English muffins, waffles or toast
chopped parsley and hard-cooked egg for garnish

Melt butter. Remove from heat and stir in flour, eliminating any lumps. Slowly stir in milk, salt and pepper; bring to a boil, stirring constantly. Combine egg yolk with white wine and lemon juice. Stir a small amount of hot milk mixture into wine mixture and then add wine mixture to hot milk. Add shellfish and simmer gently 5 minutes. Stir in chopped hard-cooked egg and Pernod. Arrange slices of avocado in crêpes or on toasted English muffins, hot waffles or toast. Spoon on the hot seafood mixture; dust with chopped parsley or sieved hard-cooked egg.
Serves 2 very generously

PAIN D'EPICES WITH VARIATIONS
Cold or toasted, it's marvelous with raspberry jam

3 cups boiling water
1-1/2 cups honey
2 cups packed brown sugar
1/4 pound butter or margarine
1 large egg, beaten
1/2 cup dark Rum
2 tablespoons Anisette
8 cups all-purpose flour, lightly spooned
  into measuring cup
1 tablespoon baking soda
1 tablespoon ground cinnamon
1/2 teaspoon salt
1 cup sliced almonds

Preheat oven to 350° and butter well 2 bread pans. Pour the boiling water over honey and brown sugar; stir in butter. When butter has melted and mixture has cooled, stir in the beaten egg, Rum and Anisette. Meanwhile, thoroughly combine flour, baking soda, cinnamon, salt and nuts in a large bowl. Stir the cooled liquid mixture into the flour mixture, combining well. Pour into pans and bake 75 to 85 minutes, until a toothpick inserted in the center comes out clean. Cool thoroughly, wrap and store. Bread will keep as long as a month. Makes 2 large loaves or 6 small ones

Variations:
• Substitute coffee for water.
• Eliminate Anisette and add another egg.
• Stir in 2 cups chopped dried fruit.

ITALIAN ANISETTE COOKIES
Crisp and dry with a light licorice flavor

3 eggs
1 cup granulated sugar
1/4 cup butter, melted
2 teaspoons anise-flavored liqueur
2-1/2 cups unsifted all-purpose flour
2 teaspoons baking powder
1 teaspoon aniseed
1/2 cup chopped almonds

Beat together eggs and sugar until very well combined. Slowly beat in melted butter and anise liqueur. Spoon flour lightly into measuring cups and sift together with baking powder into the egg mixture. Combine well, then stir in aniseed and chopped almonds. Chill for 1 hour or longer.

Grease a baking sheet and form dough into long rolls about 2 inches in diameter. If dough is too soft, work in a little more flour. Chill rolls while oven preheats to 350°. Bake whole rolls for 30 minutes, until quite firm and lightly browned. Remove from the oven and slice diagonally while on the cookie sheets. Put sheets with sliced cookies still in roll form back in the oven for 5 minutes longer. Remove from pans, separate cookies and cool on wire racks. Store in airtight containers. Do not freeze.
Makes about 6 dozen cookies

CARAWAY

Caraway/Kümmel

In Northern Europe Caraway Is a Favorite

ALL OF THE caraway-flavored liqueurs are good in cooking. Some are sweeter than others and are particularly fine for cookies, cakes and breads. The drier ones are excellent flavoring in many German, Scandinavian, Dutch or Balkan dishes, especially those featuring sauerkraut, pork or game. The flavor of caraway is pervasive and when you find it used in a liqueur, that single flavor usually dominates. For that reason it isn't listed under Herbs, Spices and Blends in this book, though often the formulas for caraway liqueurs contain other herbs as well.

Caraway seeds, borne by a plant with a big head of small flowers, have been used by man as medicine for about 2,000 years, and the Dutch have been faithful cultivators since the Middle Ages. Both Holland and Germany lay claim to originating *Kümmel,* the most famous of the caraway liqueurs. There are records of its having been made as long ago as 1575 in Amsterdam. The Dutch were fond of caraway seeds, often serving them with soft cheeses spread on rye bread. (It is still a delicious combination, as is soft cheese flavored with a caraway liqueur, then spread on thin, toasted slices of party rye.)

In the late 1690's Peter the Great of Russia worked as a carpenter in the shipyards of Amsterdam to learn European industrial techniques so that he might establish an effective Russian navy. Kümmel was one form of alcohol that warmed the mighty Russian's cold toes. He carried Kümmel back with him to Russia, stopping en route to establish Kümmel production in Latvia.

Before World War II the Wolfschmidt family of Latvia was world-famous for its excellent caraway liqueurs, particularly *Crème de Cumin.* But the war scattered the family and the Western world hasn't seen that particular Kümmel since, although Wolfschmidt is still a famous name in the spirit world, as every Vodka lover knows.

Gilka Kümmel, made in Germany, is said to be one of the finest caraway liqueurs currently on the market. *Bolskümmel* is the best known of the Dutch production today.

Aquavit, Akvavit, Akevit are three spellings for the dry spirit found in the Scandinavian countries. They are rectified potato spirit or grain neutral spirits flavored with caraway and other aromatic seeds. The name is a contraction of the Latin *aqua vitae* ("water of life").

Caraway/Kümmel

A good Danish caraway spirit is called *C.L.O.C.* (*Cumin Liquidum Optimum Castelli*—"the best caraway liqueur in the castle"). It is water-clear, as are most caraway liqueurs.

Goldwasser is an herb blend, but the dominant flavor is caraway. The gold flakes floating in the liqueur are so distinctive that it is listed separately under the chapter Gold and Silver Flakes.

Mentuccia ("a little piece of mint") comes from Italy. It is also called *Centerbe,* as it is compounded of a hundred herbs. A third name for the same caraway spirit is *Fra San Silvestro,* supposedly the name of the originator. The herbs are gathered at the foot of the Abruzzi Mountains and the combination is herby, with mint and caraway flavors the most outspoken.

PEPPY POTTED CHEESE
Use as a spread or serve on hot vegetables

3/4 pound any firm cheese you have on hand
   (sharp Cheddar is excellent)
1/4 cup caraway-flavored liqueur
1 teaspoon anise-flavored liqueur, or more to taste
1 tablespoon salad oil
1/2 teaspoon Dijon mustard
1 teaspoon coarsely ground black pepper
1 teaspoon seasoning salt, see Basics
1/2 teaspoon paprika
1/2 cup or more coarsely chopped walnuts

Grate the cheese in a blender. Empty the blender and put the liquids, mustard and seasonings in the blender; gradually add cheese and blend until smooth. Remove from blender, stir in nuts and pack into pots. Or roll the cheese into a ball and decorate the ball with chopped or whole nuts or caraway seeds. Cover tightly and store refrigerated.
Makes 2-1/2 cups

LITTLE CABBAGES SOUFFLÉ
An unusual way to serve Brussels sprouts

1/4 cup butter or margarine
1/4 cup unsifted all-purpose flour
1/2 teaspoon salt
1 cup milk
1 cup shredded Cheddar cheese
4 egg yolks
2 cups cooked Brussels sprouts, drained
   and chopped
2 tablespoons Kümmel or other caraway-
   flavored liqueur
6 egg whites
Hollandaise Sauce, see Basics (optional)

Preheat oven to 350°. In a saucepan melt butter and blend in flour and salt. Add milk gradually, stirring constantly, and cook over medium heat until mixture thickens. Add cheese, stirring until melted. Remove from heat. Beat egg yolks until thick and lemon-colored. Blend some of hot mixture into egg yolks; then blend egg yolks, chopped sprouts and liqueur into hot mixture. Return to heat and cook 3 minutes longer.

Beat egg whites until stiff but not dry; fold together with hot mixture. Turn into ungreased 2-quart soufflé dish. Bake at 350° for 30 minutes, raise to 400° for 10 minutes and then to 425° for final 5 minutes of cooking period. Serve immediately as is or with Hollandaise Sauce.
Serves 4 to 6

AQUAVIT ONIONS
A traditional holiday feast dish

1-1/2 pounds small white onions
6 tablespoons butter or margarine
6 tablespoons all-purpose flour
3 cups milk
1-1/2 teaspoons salt
1/2 teaspoon seasoning salt, see Basics
1/2 teaspoon freshly ground white pepper
2 cloves garlic, minced
1 tablespoon Aquavit
chopped parsley, bread crumbs, grated cheese
   (optional)

Cover whole, unpeeled onions with water and bring to a boil; drain and peel. Return to boiling, salted water and simmer 5 minutes or until barely tender. Drain well.

Melt butter, remove from heat and stir in flour. Gradually stir in milk and seasonings. Bring to a boil, stirring constantly to prevent lumps; then simmer 5 minutes. Add liqueur and onions. Serve as is or place in a 2-quart casserole, sprinkle with chopped parsley, bread crumbs and grated cheese and bake at 350° for 20 to 30 minutes, until nicely browned.
Makes about 6 cups

Caraway/Kümmel

SWEDISH PORK CHOPS
The caraway flavor of Kümmel
distinctively flavors this Scandinavian favorite

4 pork chops
3 scallions or shallots, thinly sliced
1/2 cup sliced fresh mushrooms
2 slices bacon, diced
1 cube beef bouillon
1/3 cup boiling water
1 teaspoon tomato paste
1 tablespoon Kümmel
1/3 cup heavy cream or half-and-half

Brown pork chops in ovenproof skillet and then add shallots and mushrooms; sauté. In another pan cook bacon bits and drain. (You may use the bacon fat to cook thick slices of raw potato to serve with the chops.) Dissolve bouillon cube in boiling water. Remove pork chops from pan and stir in bouillon, tomato paste and Kümmel, blending well. Add cream and stir to blend. Return pork chops to pan and sprinkle with bacon bits. Bake in 350° oven for 30 minutes.
Serves 2 to 4

FRANSK FISKESUPPE
Danish fish stew

1 leek or small onion, diced
2 cloves garlic, pressed or chopped
1/4 cup light olive oil
1 pound bluefish
3/4 pound flounder
4 cups water
2 tomatoes, chopped
1 teaspoon salt
1 bay leaf
a pinch of saffron
1 teaspoon grated orange rind
1 teaspoon Kümmel
1/2 pound scallops
1/4 pound shrimp, shelled and deveined
1/2 cup dry white wine
1 cup fresh, frozen or canned corn
chopped parsley

Lightly brown leek and garlic in oil. Cut fish into bone-free, bite-size pieces and add with water to pan. Stir in tomatoes, seasonings, orange rind and Kümmel. Simmer 15 minutes. Add scallops, shrimp, white wine and corn; simmer until shrimp and scallops are cooked through, about 3 to 5 minutes. Serve hot.

Let each guest sprinkle with additional Kümmel to taste. The soup can be served with buttered toast in the bottom of each bowl or accompanied by crisp, hot French bread. Garnish with parsley.
Serves 6

BALTIC RYE BREAD
Kümmel and Anisette meet rye and molasses

1 package dry yeast
1/2 cup warm water
2 cups unsifted rye flour
1/2 cup dark molasses
1/4 cup Kümmel
1 tablespoon Anisette
1/3 cup shortening
2 teaspoons salt
2 cups boiling water
6 to 7 cups unsifted all-purpose flour
1 egg, slightly beaten
caraway seed (optional)

Soften yeast in warm water. In a large bowl combine rye flour, molasses, Kümmel, Anisette, shortening and salt. Add boiling water and blend well. Cool. Add softened yeast. Gradually stir in just enough white flour to make a soft dough. Turn out onto floured surface and knead until dough is smooth and satiny (about 10 minutes), adding white flour as needed. Place in greased bowl, turning the ball of dough to oil all surfaces. Cover. Let rise in a warm place until double, about 1 hour. Punch down and shape into 3 round loaves; place on well-greased baking sheets. Let rise until double in size or until the indentation remains when finger has been pressed into loaf. Brush loaves with slightly beaten egg, covering the entire surface. Sprinkle with caraway seed, if desired. Bake in preheated 350° oven for 35 to 40 minutes.
Makes 3 plump loaves

Caraway/Kümmel

Kümmel or any caraway-flavored liqueur helps cut the fat of roast pork and with a bit of tomato paste turns the pan juices into a lovely sauce. It's an old German secret.

IRISH SEEDY BREAD
Traditional soda bread with
Kümmel and caraway seeds

4 cups unsifted all-purpose flour, spooned
  lightly into cup and leveled
1 teaspoon baking soda
1 teaspoon salt
1 teaspoon sugar
1 tablespoon Kümmel
2 tablespoons caraway seeds
1-1/2 cups buttermilk or sour milk

Preheat oven to 425°. Stir together in a bowl the flour, baking soda, salt and sugar. Add Kümmel and caraway seeds to the buttermilk; stir into flour mixture until barely combined. Turn onto a floured surface and knead lightly to shape a round loaf. Place on a lightly oiled baking sheet. Cut a deep cross on top, letting the cuts go over the sides of the bread. Bake 45 minutes or until loaf sounds hollow when tapped on the bottom.
Makes 1 loaf

SWEDISH RYE
Round loaves, glossy of crust and soft of crumb

1 package dry yeast
1/2 cup warm water
2 cups rye flour, spooned lightly into
    the cup and leveled
3/4 cup dark molasses
1/3 cup shortening
2 teaspoons salt
2 cups boiling water
1 tablespoon Kümmel
6 or more cups unsifted all-purpose flour
salad oil
1 egg, lightly beaten
caraway seeds (optional)

Soften yeast in the warm, but not scalding, water. Combine rye flour, molasses, shortening and salt; add boiling water and Kümmel. Blend well. Cool to lukewarm. Add softened yeast. Gradually stir in white flour to make a soft dough, mixing well. Turn onto a well-floured surface and knead until dough is smooth and satiny, about 10 minutes. Place in an oiled bowl and turn to grease all surfaces of the dough. Cover and let rise in a warm place until double, about 1-1/2 to 2 hours. Punch down. Cover and let rise again until almost double, about 30 minutes longer.

Turn onto lightly floured surface and divide into 3 equal parts; shape into 3 round loaves. Place on greased baking sheets, brush loaves with oil, and let rise until almost double, about 1 hour. Brush loaves with lightly beaten egg, sprinkle with caraway seeds, and bake in preheated 350° oven 35 to 40 minutes.
Makes 3 loaves

Chocolate/Cacao

All God's Children Love Chocolate

CHOCOLATE-FLAVORED liqueurs come in varying tastes—light to dark and very sweet to not-so-sweet—just as chocolate itself does. All of them combine well with any flavor that chocolate complements. Think of a box full of chocolate candies, then add a few Mexican and Spanish dishes and you've got the range.

In addition to "straight" chocolate liqueurs there are the chocolate-and-fruit or chocolate-and-mint combination liqueurs which are exactly like dipping into a candy box and pulling out a chocolate-dipped fruit nougat—only better. The liqueur is not quite so sweet, perhaps. All of the combinations are delicious over ice creams and they're wonderful news for tired dessert recipes.

The undiluted chocolate flavor of *Crème de Cacao* is a world-wide favorite. It is available either colorless, having been made by percolation of the cacao bean, or brown. Where there is color there is often a hint of vanilla flavor as well.

Royal Mint-Chocolate is a combination of delicate chocolate and mint, as is the Dutch product called *Vandermint.* All of the chocolate-mint liqueurs are luscious in any chocolate dessert. Try one of the liqueurs as a portion of the liquid in a chocolate cake batter, or in the cake's filling or frosting. Or add it to a mousse and then add a bit more to the whipped cream served with it.

Chéri-Suisse is a chocolate and cherry combination from Switzerland. It tastes like chocolate-covered cherries, only not as sweet and strident. *Chocolate Cherry* is flavored with a combination of the chocolate flavor and three different types of cherries. It is somewhat tart and adds a cheery note to cherry desserts, chocolate desserts and Cherries Jubilee.

Sabra is a subtle chocolate and Jaffa orange liqueur from Israel. It tastes much like the famed Swiss chocolate bars filled with orange liqueur. Lovely. Again, best used in desserts, and it is particularly nice in chocolate fondue sauces made for dipping bits of cake or fruit.

Chocolate Banana has a distinct banana flavor. It makes an interesting addition to a favorite banana fritter recipe.

Chocolate Raspberry is wonderful to one who spent a childhood hooked on raspberry cream candies, as I did. Ambrosia!

Baccaro Moka is a tutti-frutti treat of almond, cherry, orange, coffee, chocolate and Marsala. It comes from Sicily.

There is no end to the combinations possible and using them is a matter of tasting them, thinking about the flavor combinations and matching the liqueur flavor to a recipe.

Chocolate/Cacao

CHÉRI-SUISSE FUDGE
Blond fudge turned blushing pink

2 cups granulated sugar
1 cup heavy cream
1 tablespoon light corn syrup
1/2 teaspoon salt
2 tablespoons butter
1 tablespoon Chéri-Suisse
1/4 cup chopped maraschino cherries
1/4 cup coarsely chopped nuts

Butter sides of a heavy 2-quart saucepan. In it combine sugar, cream, corn syrup and salt. Cook over medium heat, stirring constantly, until the sugar dissolves and mixture comes to a full boil. Stop stirring. Cook to soft ball stage (about 238°). Immediately remove from heat and cool to luke-warm without stirring. Add butter and Chéri-Suisse. Beat vigorously until mixture becomes very thick and begins to lose its gloss. Quickly stir in cherries and nuts. Drop from a teaspoon or spread in a buttered 9x5-inch pan. Score while warm; cut when cool and firm.
Makes about 12 good-size pieces

CHOCOLATE-MINT PIE
Simple to make and pretty as a picture

Crust:
16 Hydrox cookies, crushed
5 tablespoons butter or margarine

Filling:
24 marshmallows
1/3 cup milk
1 cup heavy cream, whipped
1 ounce (2 tablespoons) green Crème de Menthe
1 ounce (2 tablespoons) white Crème de Cacao

Crust: Preheat oven to 350°. Combine crumbs with butter and press into a 9-inch pie pan. Bake 10 minutes. Cool.
Filling: Heat marshmallows and milk in the top of a double boiler until the marshmallows melt and can be stirred into the milk. Cool well; then fold in whipped cream and liqueurs. Pour into pie shell and refrigerate. Serve with more whipped cream, if you wish, and decorate with chocolate curls (made by running a potato peeler over a square of baking chocolate).
Serves 6 to 8

CRÈME DE CACAO BREAD
A cake-like quick bread

1/4 pound butter or margarine
3/4 cup granulated sugar
2 eggs
1-1/2 cups unsifted all-purpose flour, spooned
   into cup and leveled
1 teaspoon salt
2 teaspoons baking powder
3 tablespoons chopped walnuts
1/3 cup milk
1/3 cup Crème de Cacao
2 tablespoons presweetened instant cocoa powder

Preheat oven to 350°. Butter and lightly flour 1-quart mold or 9-inch square baking pan. Cream together butter, sugar and eggs until light and fluffy. Combine flour, salt, baking powder and nuts. Add to creamed mixture alternately with milk which has been mixed with Crème de Cacao; completely combine after each addition. Spoon 1/3 of the batter into the mold, spreading some of the batter up the sides. Sprinkle 1/2 of the cocoa over the batter. Spoon on additional batter and run a knife through to somewhat blend cocoa and batter. Add remaining cocoa, top with remaining batter and again run a knife through the batter. Bake 40 minutes or until it tests done. Let stand 10 minutes or longer before turning out of mold. Serve warm.
Makes 1 loaf

CHOCOLATE ICING
Fudge-like without the nuisance factor

2-1/2 cups sifted confectioners' sugar
1 egg
2 tablespoons water
1/4 cup granulated sugar
1/4 teaspoon salt
2 squares unsweetened chocolate
1/4 pound butter or margarine
1 teaspoon Crème de Cacao

Beat together confectioners' sugar and egg until light and fluffy. In a saucepan combine water, granulated sugar, salt and chocolate. Place over low heat and stir until chocolate is melted and ingredients are blended. Raise heat to medium and bring mixture to a boil, stirring constantly; boil gently 1 minute. Remove from heat and add butter and Crème de Cacao, stirring until blended. Add egg mixture and beat until creamy.
Makes enough to generously cover
top and sides of a 2-layer cake

Citrus fruits

Citrus Fruits

The Orange Is So A-Peeling!

CITRUS-BASED LIQUEURS have proven to be both popular and proliferating. All of them, whether flavored by orange, tangerine, lemon, lime or grapefruit, are marvelous in cooking.

The orange and tangerine flavors automatically enhance virtually any fruit dish, be it crisp and fresh or cooked and soft. They are excellent flavoring for whipped cream, delicious in chocolate desserts, and they maintain extremely friendly relations with duckling, ham, pork and wild game. They are so versatile you will probably find it more economical to invest in large bottles and keep them under lock and key than to buy them in miniatures.

ORANGE

Most orange-flavored liqueurs are made from the peel of oranges; the flesh goes elsewhere. It is important that the oranges be gathered at the correct time as green peel has a different flavor from that of ripe fruit. Brand flavors come from the types of peel used; some are bitter and others are not. Each maker blends to give his product its own special taste.

Curaçao originally was made only with fruit from the island of Curaçao, but the term has become generic. It is used for orange-flavored liqueurs made almost anywhere, with oranges from such close "anywheres" as Israel and Algeria putting their peels into the same distilling pots. Curaçaos come in a rainbow of colors—orange, brown, white, blue and green.

Cointreau is made in Angers, in the heart of the French fruit country, where the Cointreau company originated. Many other liqueurs are made by this company from local fruits, but Cointreau is a blend of five different peels imported from around the world.

Grand Marnier is an orange liqueur distinguished by the fact that its base is entirely Cognac.

Picon, a French combination of orange with quinine, is bitter and not really recommended for use in cooking.

Sabra, made in Israel, is a blend of chocolate and orange flavors. For chocolate liqueur cooking suggestions see Chocolate/Cacao.

Van der Hum is an interesting South African liqueur made of an orange-type fruit—the naartjies—and flavored with other fruits, plants, seeds and barks. It was an attempt on the part of the homesick Dutch settlers to reproduce their favorite Curaçao. The name originated because the settlers were unable to remember the name of the inventor. They called it the Dutch equivalent of "Mr. What's-His-Name."

Citrus Fruits

Aurum is produced in Pescara, Italy, from fresh oranges, aromatic and medicinal herbs, seeds, roots and plants. The base is aged Italian Brandy.

TANGERINES

Crème de Mandarine and other liqueurs obtained from the dried peel of tangerines are made by the Dutch, French and Danes . . . probably others as well. *Mandarine Napoléon* is a Belgian spirit based upon Cognac and Andalusian tangerine distillates. It is said to have been a favorite of both Napoleon and Josephine who saw to it that the Belgians got all of the Cognac they needed for its production. Tangerine-flavored liqueurs can be used almost interchangeably with orange liqueurs and are particularly appropriate when tangerines are an ingredient in the recipe.

LEMON AND LIME

Lemon and lime Gins and Vodkas are popular in Britain and there are various lemon liqueurs around the world, although few, if any, are made in the United States. *Kitron* is a Greek spirit distilled from grape Brandy and the leaves of the lemon tree.

Lemon and Fruit and *Lime and Fruit* are a part of an "and Fruit" series where fruit flavors are combined, with one of the flavors speaking more loudly than others. They are used wherever a bouquet of fruit flavors would be welcome, as in fruit salads, compotes, etc.

CITRUS BLENDS

Exotic, sweet *Parfait Amour* is a citrus-oil liqueur flavored with flower petals and made in several colors, the most startling of which are inky blue and bright violet. It doesn't sound appetizing and it doesn't look appetizing, but love is blind, and you can sometimes slip it in where the color won't matter, as in candies.

Passion Fruit is deep gold in color (not purple as you might suspect) and citrus in flavor.

Rock and Rye is made by steeping citrus and other fruits in Rye Whiskey. Check the Whiskey and Whisky section of the Liquor chapter for recipes.

GRAPEFRUIT

The grapefruit-based liqueurs are interesting to experiment with. They are fine additions to salad dressings (particularly those used on fruit, fruit-and-vegetable and some seafood salads), as a part of the liquid in molded salads and in sorbets. They are popular in Australia and in the Caribbean (perhaps because they are flavor-mates with Rum), but hard to find in the United States. Rum, apricot liqueurs or any of the citrus liqueurs will turn plain-Jane grapefruit into a fancy dessert or appetizer if you spoon it over the fruit, let it stand for a while and then broil.

CALIFORNIA BREAD
*Rum and orange-flavored liqueur
bring out the fruit flavors*

2 cups granulated sugar
4 cups unsifted all-purpose flour, spooned
   lightly into cup and leveled
2 teaspoons baking powder
1 teaspoon salt
1 cup chopped dates
1 cup chopped dried apricots
1 cup chopped walnuts
2 eggs
1-1/4 cups orange juice
1/4 cup orange-flavored liqueur
1/2 cup dark Rum
2 teaspoons baking soda
2 tablespoons butter or margarine, melted

Preheat oven to 350°. In a large mixing bowl stir together the sugar, flour, baking powder and salt. Mix in dates, apricots and walnuts. In another bowl beat eggs and combine with remaining ingredients in the order listed. Add the wet ingredients to the dry and stir just until combined; do not overmix. Pour into 2 well-greased bread pans and bake 1 hour and 10 minutes or until a toothpick inserted in center of loaf comes out clean.
Makes 2 loaves

PLEASE DO EAT THE BASKET
A simple batter that bakes into a shell

2 eggs
1/2 cup unsifted all-purpose flour, spooned
   lightly into cup and leveled
1/2 teaspoon salt
1/2 cup milk
2 tablespoons butter, melted
confectioners' sugar
2 cups fruit of choice, marinated with
   sugar and any fruit- or mint-flavored liqueur
1 cup sour cream
orange-flavored liqueur

Preheat oven to 450°. Beat eggs and add flour, salt and milk; beat smooth. Stir in butter. Pour into greased 9-inch ovenproof skillet and bake on bottom shelf of oven 20 minutes. Reduce heat to 350° and prick the shell if necessary (there may be a large bubble or two). Bake 10 minutes longer. Remove from frypan to a warm platter. Sprinkle the inside of bottom with confectioners' sugar. Spoon marinated fruit into the shell. Flavor the sour cream with orange-flavored liqueur and spoon in the center of the fruit. Top with a pretty piece of fruit and sprinkle on more confectioners' sugar. Serve while the shell is hot.
Serves 6

Citrus Fruits

RING AROUND THE STRAWBERRIES CAKE
Elegant and easy

Gateau:
4 tablespoons butter
1 cup granulated sugar
grated rind of 1 orange (about 1 tablespoon)
2 large eggs, separated
1-1/2 cups sifted all-purpose flour
1-1/2 teaspoons baking powder
1/2 teaspoon salt
1/2 cup milk
1 tablespoon orange-flavored liqueur

Filling:
1 quart fresh strawberries
strawberry jam
strawberry jelly

Frosting:
1/2 pint heavy cream
1/3 cup granulated sugar
1 tablespoon plus 1 teaspoon orange-
 flavored liqueur
1/3 cup sliced almonds, toasted

Gateau: Butter and lightly flour the bottom of two 9-inch cake pans (cover non-removable bottoms with greased waxed paper). Preheat oven to 350°. Cream together butter, sugar and grated orange rind. Add egg yolks one at a time and beat well after each addition. Sift flour, baking powder and salt together; combine milk with liqueur. Gently stir about 1/3 of flour mixture into creamed mixture. Blend in half of the liquid; then another 1/3 of flour; add the remaining liquid and end with the flour mixture. Stir no more than necessary to combine ingredients. Beat egg whites until stiff and carefully fold them into the cake batter. Pour into greased pans and bake 25 minutes or until done. Cool 5 minutes. Remove from pans; cool on racks.
Filling: When the cake is cool, cut the center out of 1 layer, leaving a rim about 1 inch wide. Reserve center circle for other use. Spread strawberry jam over the other layer and place the cake rim on top. Melt sufficient strawberry jelly (flavored with Framboise or Kirsch if you wish) to glaze the strawberries. While jelly is melting arrange whole, fresh berries to fill the area within the rim. Spoon melted jelly over them to glaze.
Frosting: Whip the cream, gradually adding the sugar. As it begins to stiffen, add liqueur. Frost the rim and sides of the cake. Sprinkle liberally with toasted almonds (throw them against the sides and they will stay in place). Refrigerate until served.
Serves 8 to 12

GERMAN PANCAKE
Like a giant crêpe it can hold untold treasures;
serve it for breakfast, lunch or as a dessert

1 tablespoon butter
1 egg, beaten
2 tablespoons sugar
pinch salt
2-1/2 tablespoons flour
1/4 cup milk
1 teaspoon orange-flavored or any fruit-
    flavored liqueur

Melt butter in a heavy 8- to 10-inch ovenproof skillet. In order listed, measure remaining ingredients into a jar, cover tightly and shake until just blended. Pour into skillet and place in cold oven. Start oven and bake at extremely hot (550°) temperature until pancake is puffy and cooked throughout, about 20 minutes. Slide out onto a platter, fill and fold two sides over center.

    To freeze, fold cooked pancakes in thirds and wrap in foil. To serve, heat in 500° oven for 10 minutes.
Serves 2 or more

Filling Suggestions: Any fruit or combination of whole or mashed fruits such as pineapple, oranges, nectarines, bananas, apples or berries. For a breakfast entrée fill with scrambled eggs.

Citrus Fruits

POLISH BABKA
A cross between bread and cake,
flavored with Rum and orange

1-1/4 cups milk
2 packages dry yeast
1/2 cup warm water
5 cups unsifted all-purpose flour, spooned
    into a cup and leveled
1/4 pound soft butter or margarine
1/2 cup granulated sugar
2 eggs
1 teaspoon salt
1 tablespoon orange-flavored liqueur
1 tablespoon Rum (either light or dark)
3/4 to 1 cup raisins or currants
1 tablespoon butter, melted
3 tablespoons fine dry bread crumbs
Icing for Polish Babka, following

Heat milk until bubbles form around edge of pan; cool to lukewarm. In a large bowl dissolve yeast in water. Stir in milk and 2 cups flour; beat until smooth and satiny. Beat in butter and sugar. Add eggs, one at a time, beating well after each addition. Beat in salt, liqueur, Rum and remaining flour. Beat until batter is smooth and sheets from spoon or beater. Stir in raisins. Cover. Let rise until double in bulk, about 1-1/2 hours. Beat down; cover and let rise again about 1 hour.

Brush 10-inch tube pan with melted butter; sprinkle with crumbs. Beat risen batter to deflate it; spoon into prepared pan. Let rise again until double in bulk, about 1 hour. Bake in preheated 325° oven for 30 minutes, then increase to 350° for 25 minutes. Remove from oven; let stand in pan 10 minutes. Turn out and ice while warm.
Makes 1 large cake

ICING FOR POLISH BABKA

1/2 cup sifted confectioners' sugar
2 teaspoons heavy cream
1 teaspoon orange-flavored liqueur

Combine ingredients and spread over warm Babka. Frosting should be fairly thick as the heat will cause it to run gently down the sides like raindrops on an April day—or legs in a wine glass.

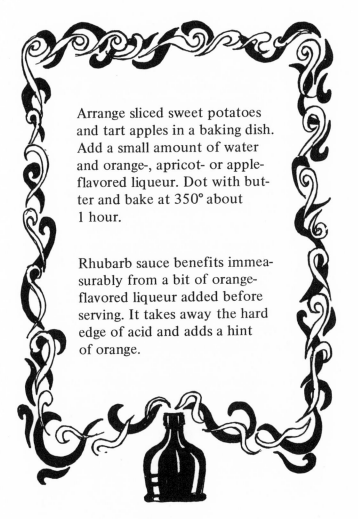

Arrange sliced sweet potatoes and tart apples in a baking dish. Add a small amount of water and orange-, apricot- or apple-flavored liqueur. Dot with butter and bake at 350° about 1 hour.

Rhubarb sauce benefits immeasurably from a bit of orange-flavored liqueur added before serving. It takes away the hard edge of acid and adds a hint of orange.

BERRY BREAD
Serve as a sweet bread or as a base for shortcake

1 cup all-purpose flour, spooned lightly into
    cup and leveled
1 teaspoon ground cinnamon
1/2 teaspoon baking soda
1/2 teaspoon salt
2/3 cup granulated sugar
2/3 cup crushed unsweetened berries, fresh
    or frozen
2 small eggs, well beaten
1/3 cup plus 1 tablespoon cooking oil
1 teaspoon orange-flavored or other liqueur
    (depending on fruit used)*

Preheat oven to 350°. Grease and flour a 1-pound coffee can or a bread pan. Sift or lightly stir the first 4 ingredients together in a large mixing bowl. Beat together the last 5 ingredients and mix into dry ingredients just until combined. Pour into can or pan, filling about half full. Bake 1 hour.
Makes 1 loaf

*Note: Orange is very nice with most any berry, as is Kirsch. Cassis is a natural with blueberries. But any fresh fruit and fruit-flavored liqueur combination is worth exploring. Then, too, there is Rum.

Citrus Fruits

SABRA-CHOCOLATE SAUCE
A double-chocolate smoothie

24 ounces semisweet chocolate
1/2 cup Sabra
1/2 cup water or coffee
1-1/2 cups chopped walnuts (optional)

Combine all ingredients except nuts in a double boiler; cook, stirring occasionally, until a smooth sauce is formed. Stir in nuts. Pour into sterile jars with self-sealing caps or store, covered, in the refrigerator. Serve warm or at room temperature.
Makes 2-2/3 cups

APRICOT HARD SAUCE
Hard to resist—good on fruitcake or
hot mince, apple or apricot pie

1/4 pound soft butter or margarine
2 cups confectioners' sugar
1/2 cup apricot preserves
orange-flavored liqueur to taste

Beat butter until fluffy; gradually beat in sugar. Stir in preserves and liqueur. Chill until serving time.
Makes about 2 cups

BLUEBERRY CLOUD PIE
Cassis or an orange-based liqueur
makes this heavenly

pastry for a single-crust pie, see Basics
1 cup granulated sugar
2 tablespoons all-purpose flour
1/4 teaspoon salt
1 tablespoon lemon juice
1 tablespoon orange-flavored liqueur or Cassis
3 eggs, separated
3 cups fresh or frozen blueberries
2 tablespoons confectioners' sugar
1 tablespoon orange-flavored liqueur

Preheat oven to 425°. Prepare 1 recipe Basic Pastry and use 1/4 of dough for shell; refrigerate or freeze remainder. Roll out dough as directed in recipe and line an 8- or 9-inch pie pan. Pierce shell with tines of fork and bake at 425° for 10 to 12 minutes. Cool.

Lower oven to 350°. If using fresh berries, remove stems. In a double boiler combine granulated sugar, flour, salt, lemon juice, 1 tablespoon orange-flavored liqueur or Cassis, egg yolks and blueberries. Cook over medium-low heat until mixture thickens, about 10 minutes, stirring occasionally to prevent lumping. Beat egg whites until stiff, gradually beating in confectioners' sugar and 1 tablespoon orange-flavored liqueur. Pour berry mixture into baked pie shell and mound meringue over filling, spreading to anchor to crust on all sides. Bake 15 minutes or until lightly touched with gold.
Serves 6

SWEET-TART FRUIT SAUCE
Gooseberries and strawberries
make a good marriage

1 cup water
2 tablespoons cornstarch
2 cups fresh, frozen or canned gooseberries, stemmed
2 cups sliced fresh or frozen strawberries, hulled
1 tablespoon orange-flavored liqueur
1-1/2 cups granulated sugar
1/4 teaspoon salt

Stir together 1/3 cup water and 2 tablespoons cornstarch. When there are no lumps gradually add to remaining water in a saucepan. Bring to a boil, stirring constantly. Add gooseberries, strawberries and liqueur. Continue to simmer. Stir in sugar and salt to taste. Serve as a cold soup or as a sauce. Sour cream is very nice with either, particularly if it is sprinkled with grated orange peel.
Serves 8

Coffee and Tea

Blends with the Bean and the Leaf

COFFEE LIQUEURS will enhance any flavor that goes well with a cup of coffee. Like many liqueurs, they add glamour to unsweetened whipped cream and the cream seems appropriate spooned onto fresh gingerbread, brownies, or anything in the world made of chocolate. Combined with chocolate in a recipe, the coffee flavor becomes a lovely mocha taste. For a surprising dessert, make your favorite mousse recipe using white chocolate instead of dark chocolate and flavor it with coffee-flavored liqueur. Delicious.

But desserts aren't the only use for coffee-flavored liqueurs. They add an unusual accent to pork and ham preparations and to duck and venison dishes as well. You don't really taste the coffee—but you do taste the difference.

Tia Maria is a Jamaican Rum-based liqueur blended with Blue Mountain coffee extracts and local spices. The fairy tale that goes with this Caribbean favorite has it that when Jamaica was invaded by the British in 1655 the Spanish families fled their homes. In the chaos a beautiful girl became separated from her family. A faithful servant named Tia Maria saved the secret recipe for the family cordial and the young lady. The senorita subsequently married a dashing British officer and dashed off a large family. When her eldest daughter married she was given the recipe saved by, and named for, Tia Maria. When the girl capitalized on her dowry isn't recorded, but Tia Maria is a nice legacy for us to cook with.

Kahlúa is a popular Mexican coffee liqueur whose fame rests not upon legend, but upon its importance in the Black Russian cocktail. At one time it went to market in ceramic bottles resembling Aztec carvings.

Pasha, another coffee liqueur, is made in Turkey and marketed in exotic bottles which look as though they may be modeled after hammered copper. The flavor base for Pasha is dark-roasted Turkish coffee.

The Irish, having discovered the great popularity of Irish coffee, now make *Irish Coffee Liqueur,* a combination of Irish Whiskey, coffee and honey.

Sa'ala coffee liqueur is said to have originated in the 1830's in Algeria. The Zouaves (French-Algerian soldiers famed for their colorful costumes, carefree lifestyles and courage) felt it gave them the strength for all three. The base is Cognac.

Coffee and Tea

Expresso Coffee Liqueur is an Italian import with the same slightly bitter undertone of espresso coffee. A caffeine-free *Expresso* is also available.

El Toro is said to be made from espresso and has that same slightly bitter undertone.

Coffee and Brandy is Colombian coffee blended with California Brandy. *Crème de Café* is a sweeter Colombian coffee liqueur.

Never to be outdone, the Swiss produce *Marmot* in three flavors—chocolate, café and mocha. The chocolate and café blends both have tiny pieces of chocolate floating in the liqueur. The mocha has whole coffee beans afloat.

Austria supplies us with *Viennese Coffee Liqueur*. *Expresso Galacafé* has the strong flavor of Italian espresso coffee and *Mayan Coffee Liqueur* is flavored with Mexican coffee beans.

TEA

While they're not made from a bean, and haven't been too successful on the American market, there are liqueurs based upon tea. One is *Ceylonese Tea Liqueur,* another an Austrian favorite called *Tea Atomizer* and Suntory of Japan makes a *Green Tea Liqueur.* All are blends of teas and herbs, just as most flavored teas, blended for steeping in boiling water, are blends of teas, herbs and flowers. In cooking they would be used as you would an herb-blend liqueur (see chapter on Herbs, Spices and Blends).

BITTERSWEET MOCHA SAUCE
Any of the coffee liqueurs can be used

1 6-ounce package semisweet chocolate
1 1-ounce square unsweetened chocolate, melted
2 to 3 tablespoons coffee-flavored liqueur
1/2 cup heavy cream

Combine chocolate and 2 tablespoons of liqueur in top of double boiler. When chocolate has melted, gradually stir in cream. For a thinner sauce add another tablespoon of liqueur. Serve hot.
Makes 3/4 cup

LUSCIOUS MOCHA SAUCE
Marvelous on coffee or peppermint ice cream

24 ounces semisweet chocolate
1/2 cup coffee-flavored or chocolate- and coffee-
   flavored liqueur
1/2 cup water or coffee
1-1/2 cups chopped walnuts, pecans or pistachios

Combine all ingredients except nuts in a double boiler; stir occasionally until a smooth sauce is formed. Stir in nuts. Serve warm.
Makes 2-2/3 cups

BLACK RUSSIAN PIE
Instead of drinking a Black Russian, you eat one

1/3 cup Kahlúa or other coffee-flavored liqueur
2 packets unflavored gelatin
1/2 cup milk, heated to boiling
2 eggs
1/2 cup granulated sugar
2/3 cup Vodka
1-1/2 cups heavy cream
Kahlúa Crumb Crust, following
whipped cream and candied mint leaves for garnish

Run the first 3 ingredients in a blender or stir together well until the gelatin is dissolved. Beat in eggs, sugar and Vodka; chill 15 minutes until slightly thickened, stirring occasionally to keep smooth. Whip cream and fold together with gelatin mixture. Pour into Kahlúa Crumb Crust and chill until set, about 1 hour. Garnish with more whipped cream and candied mint leaves.
Serves 6 to 8

KAHLÚA CRUMB CRUST
Good with any cream pie filling,
but especially designed for the Black Russian

16 graham crackers or 20 chocolate wafers,
  crushed (1 cup crumbs)
4 tablespoons butter or margarine, melted
2 tablespoons Kahlúa or other
  coffee-flavored liqueur

Combine crumbs with butter and liqueur. Press onto bottom and sides of an 8-inch pie pan. Chill 30 minutes before filling.
Makes 1 crust

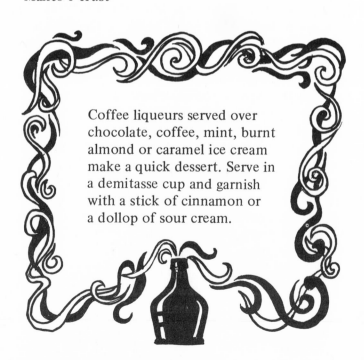

Coffee liqueurs served over chocolate, coffee, mint, burnt almond or caramel ice cream make a quick dessert. Serve in a demitasse cup and garnish with a stick of cinnamon or a dollop of sour cream.

CHOCOLATE-MOCHA ROLL
Coffee liqueur flavors roll and filling;
Rum flavors the icing

4 large eggs, separated
1/2 teaspoon cream of tartar
1/2 cup sifted confectioners' sugar
4 tablespoons unsweetened cocoa powder
1 teaspoon coffee-flavored liqueur
1/8 teaspoon salt
Coffee Cream, following
Pistachio-Rum Icing, following

Preheat oven to 325°. Line a shallow 8x12-inch pan with heavy paper (parchment works well) and oil the paper lining. Beat egg whites with cream of tartar until stiff, but not dry; set aside. Beat egg yolks and gradually add sugar, cocoa, coffee-flavored liqueur and salt. Fold into stiffly beaten egg whites. Spread evenly over oiled paper and bake 20 minutes. While the cake is baking dampen a tea towel and sprinkle one side heavily with confectioners' sugar. When the cake is removed from the oven, loosen cake around the sides and invert onto the tea towel. Remove pan and carefully peel off paper. Roll cake in towel and let it cool (it can be left overnight if you wish) before filling and frosting.
Serves 8 to 10

COFFEE CREAM
A not-too-sweet filling

1 cup heavy cream
3 tablespoons coffee-flavored liqueur

Whip cream and fold in 1 tablespoon of the liqueur at a time. Unroll cake and spread with the cream. Reroll and refrigerate while making the frosting.

PISTACHIO-RUM ICING
Flavored with Rum, cocoa and coffee

4 tablespoons butter or margarine
1 cup sifted confectioners' sugar
1 tablespoon unsweetened cocoa powder
1/8 teaspoon salt
1-1/2 tablespoons strong coffee
2 teaspoons dark Rum
1/4 cup chopped pistachio nuts

Cream butter and gradually add sugar, cocoa, salt and coffee; beat 2 minutes. Stir in Rum. Spread over top of Chocolate Roll with Coffee Cream Filling and sprinkle the surface with chopped pistachios.

Flowers

𝔉𝔩𝔬𝔴𝔢𝔯𝔰

Bouquets of Flavors

FLOWER FLAVORS—orange blossoms and rose blossoms particularly—are used extensively in Middle Eastern cooking, and even the English enjoy jasmine tea. The use of liqueurs flavored with flowers is almost exclusively limited to desserts. They're a pleasant surprise lightly sprinkled on fresh berries or pound cake.

The lore of liqueurs has it that in 15th century Padua a doctor was pestered by a rich lady hypochondriac. He, being a clever man, combined Brandy, honey and a perfume extracted from roses. The honey sweetened her tongue, the Brandy her disposition and the roses her breath. She sweetened his bank account, and the flower-flavored liqueurs were born.

Rose petal-flavored liqueurs are still popular in Italy. Pink *Crème de Roses* produced in France is exported chiefly to the Mediterranean market.

Fior d'Alpe (Alpine flowers), *Isolabella, Edelweis* and *Millefiori* are Italian liqueurs which are said to contain the extracts of thousands of flowers. They used to be shipped in tall, fluted bottles containing small twigs hung with sugar crystals. The crystals were deposited as the liqueur, which was bottled warm, slowly cooled. The process has caused difficulties with importation into the United States as the alcoholic strength varies due to the bottling-while-warm procedure. Sadly, the crystal-draped twig has been replaced with plastic fern. These liqueurs are more herby than flowery in taste, smooth and interesting in desserts and in vegetable dishes which can tolerate sweetness.

Crème de Violette is also very sweet, made from real violets and colored to match its name. *Crème Yvette* is a Parma violet liqueur also violet in color and named to honor the French actress Yvette Gilbert. It was very popular in the United States at one time in a cocktail named "The Blue Moon."

Cherry Blossom Liqueur is a Japanese favorite.

Flower-flavored liqueurs taste very much like the flowers smell. They're quite unusual and hard to find in some areas.

PINEAPPLE GARNISH
FOR ROAST DUCK OR HAM

*This is lovely for people who don't like
sweet sauces with meat. Not too sweet, it makes
a lovely dessert topped with
whipped cream flavored with the liqueur*

1 8-ounce can pineapple slices (in their own
   juice, no sugar added), drained
1 tablespoon packed light brown sugar
Fior d'Alpe, Rum or Bourbon to taste

Arrange pineapple slices in a shallow baking dish.
Combine sugar with spirit and pour over the slices.
Run under broiler briefly to heat and glaze.

Serve Crème de Violette over
lemon sherbet and garnish with
candied violets.

HEAVENLY HAM LOAF
Easy to make and the flavor is ethereal

Loaf:
1 pound bulk pork sausage
1/2 pound ground ham (2 cups)
3 bread slices, torn (2 cups)
1 small onion, chopped
1/4 cup chopped parsley
1 egg
1 tablespoon Fior d'Alpe or Galliano
milk
1/2 teaspoon dry mustard

Glaze:
1/4 cup packed brown sugar
1 teaspoon Fior d'Alpe or Galliano
1 tablespoon frozen orange juice concentrate
1/4 teaspoon dry mustard

Place meats, bread, onion and parsley in a bowl.
Break egg into a measuring cup; add liqueur and
pour in milk to make 1/2 cup. Add mustard and
beat to combine. Pour into meat mixture and
squeeze together with your hands to make a
smooth, well-combined mixture. Press into a loaf
pan and spread the top with combined Glaze
ingredients. Bake 1 hour in a 350° oven.
Serves 4 to 6

Fruit—Pits and Pulp

Please Do Squeeze the Bottles!

PROBABLY the most popular of the liqueurs and by far the most useful in cooking are the fruit flavors. They smell good, taste good and cook good. They just naturally make anything they go into "good-er."

The fruit flavors fall into two big categories: unsweetened distillates of the fruits called *eaux de vie*, *white alcohols* or *fruit Brandies* and those that are sweetened, i.e. liqueurs or cordials such as *crèmes* and *fruit-flavored Brandies*.

EAUX DE VIE, WHITE ALCOHOLS OR FRUIT BRANDIES

If soft fruits are mashed, fermented and then heated, alcohol is driven off. When the vapor is collected and bottled, a clear alcohol with the distinctive flavor of the fruit is produced.

These products are called: eaux de vie (water of life), white alcohols (because they are clear and colorless) or fruit Brandies (which they truly are). Examples are: *Kirsch* (cherry pulp and pits), *Prune* or *Prunelle* (plum), *Quetsch* (Swiss plum and pits), *Mirabelle* (Mirabelle plum), *Fraise* (strawberry), *Fraise de Bois* (wild strawberry), *Framboise* (raspberry), *Poire* (pear) and *Barack Palinka* (apricot).

They are lovely to cook with and have delightful aromas. The stone fruit Brandies, such as Kirsch and Quetsch, have a fine bitter tang from the crushed kernels in the fermenting fruit juice. These water-white Brandies cannot be aged in wood, as this would give them color and alter the flavor. They are bottled soon after distillation and should not be kept too long as their flavors tend to lessen with age. Buy them in small quantities when you can. They are all excellent in marinating fruits, flavoring whipped cream and sauces and in cooking any meat which takes kindly to the corresponding fruit—duckling and Kirsch (cherries) would be an example, pork and Barack Palinka (apricots) another.

FRUIT-FLAVORED BRANDIES AND CRÈMES

"Fruit-flavored" Brandies are normally made by macerating the fruit in grape Brandy (or in another spirit) and adding some sugar. Often some of the more expensive eau de vie is added to enhance the aroma and flavor. They are generally colored rather than clear and of higher proof than most other liqueurs.

70

Hence, fruit-flavored Brandies are sweeter and less expensive than the eaux de vie and are an entirely different product. They, too, are excellent in cooking, particularly where their sweetness can be a welcome addition to fruit breads, desserts, puddings and fruit salads. Crèmes and Polish-style liqueurs are both sweeter than fruit-flavored Brandies and are best used in desserts.

Warning to travelers: Outside the United States liqueurs are often called Brandies. In England Apricot Brandy would not mean an eau de vie but instead a sweet apricot liqueur!

Apple

Applejack and *Apple Brandy* are synonymous terms, but *Calvados* means something else again. The chief distinction is the aging. Calvados, which comes from the town of Calvados, Normandy, in the center of France's apple and cider production area, is generally sold after it has aged in wood ten years, and is usually 90° proof. Our Applejack or Apple Brandy has usually been aged two to five years in wood and is 100° proof. The oak barrels add color and flavor to the spirits and the longer they rest in the barrel the greater the change and the higher the price. A definite apple flavor remains in both.

Any bottle labeled Calvados will be relatively dry and is a natural flavoring ingredient with apple desserts (either in the dish itself or in the cream or sauce that goes on top). Calvados is excellent with pork or duckling (it helps to break down the natural fat) and with wild game such as duck, goose, venison and hare. Brush the bird's body cavity with Calvados before stuffing and then baste with a mixture of Calvados and butter. Add Calvados to an apple stuffing for game, ham or pork (including suckling pig).

Apple-flavored Brandy and Apple Brandy are both sweeter than Calvados, but not as fruity as *Hard Cider*. Hard Cider is not distilled and generally is sweeter than either Calvados or Applejack. It is excellent in cooking pork or game.

Fruit—Pits and Pulp

TIPPLED RUM-APPLE RINGS
A glamorous version of baked apples

7 large cooking apples
3/4 cup well-packed light brown sugar
3 tablespoons sweet butter
1/4 cup light Rum
additional Rum

Crème Chantilly:
1 cup heavy cream
4 teaspoons Calvados
2 tablespoons granulated sugar

Preheat oven to 450°. Peel and core apples, leaving them whole. Slice into thin rings and reshape into whole apples again. When you've done them all, make 2 equal-sized stacks of rings, discarding the smaller pieces from the ends so that the slices used are fairly uniform in size. (The discarded parts may reward the cook for his efforts or be used for applesauce or in a stuffing later on.) Place the 2 stacks on edge, side by side on a well-buttered baking dish just large enough to hold them. Gently tip the apples over domino-fashion and sprinkle with brown sugar. Dot with butter and trickle 1/4 cup Rum over all. Bake 30 minutes; baste and reduce heat to 350° for an additional 20 minutes, basting several times more. Be careful not to let the beautiful syrup boil dry. Remove from the oven and lightly sprinkle with additional Rum.
Crème Chantilly: Whip cream; beat in sugar and Calvados. Serve with apple rings.
Serves 4 or 5
72

SUCKLING PIG

A shoat (young pig, just after weaning) has lovely skin, almost like a baby's, but before he is stuffed the hair must be removed. It can either be singed off or shaved away with a safety razor. When he is smooth and hairless wash him off and out, then proceed with the stuffing.

Once dried his body cavity should be rubbed with salt and sage moistened with Calvados or Applejack. Then the Savory Sausage Stuffing (following) goes in. Some ovens may not be large enough to accommodate the little fellow, but if you tuck his hind legs up under his chin and truss them to his forelegs, a 24-inch oven will do nicely for a 4- to 6-week-old shoat (about 13 pounds). Boned (except for legs, hooves and head), a piglet can be roasted in an even smaller space.

The stuffed shoat should be placed on a rack resting over a foil-lined roasting pan. Turn the bottom foil up loosely around the piglet. Cover his ears and tail with foil and place either a tightly rolled ball of foil or a child's wooden block in his mouth. Then cover the whole shoat with foil or with wet cooking parchment.

A piglet will require about 25 minutes cooking time per pound at 350°. During the last hour of cooking remove the foil and baste every 5 or 10 minutes to produce a crackling skin. Combine equal quantities of white wine and melted butter for basting and use the pan drippings as well. The pork is done when a skewer inserted into the thickest part of the meat brings forth a spurt of fat rather than a watery liquid. Once out of the oven blue marbles may be used for eyes or olives can be inserted. Replace the ball of foil with a shiny red apple and carry your succulent friend off for his grand entrance. Serve with Giblet Sauce, following.

SAVORY SAUSAGE STUFFING
Equally good with suckling pig or turkey

2 pounds country sausage
2 large onions, chopped
2 large cloves garlic, minced or pressed
4 cups torn raisin bread
4 cups torn white bread
2 apples, cored and chopped but not peeled
1 cup black walnuts, chopped
1 tablespoon salt
2 teaspoons freshly ground pepper
2 teaspoons thyme
5 eggs
1/4 cup Calvados or Applejack

In a large frying pan sauté the sausage, onion and garlic, breaking the meat into small bits as it cooks. Add the torn breads, apple, walnuts and seasonings. Beat eggs and spirit together, then stir into meat mixture. Stuff very loosely into the body cavity and sew or skewer tightly.
Makes enough to stuff a 13-pound shoat
or a large turkey

Note: The liver, heart and kidneys may be simmered then chopped fine, sautéed in butter, seasoned and added to the stuffing, or these giblets can be used to make a sauce, following.

GIBLET SAUCE
*A rich sauce to accompany
suckling pig or roast turkey*

liver, heart and kidneys from piglet or turkey
1/4 pound butter or margarine
1 small onion, finely chopped
1-1/2 cups heavy cream
2 teaspoons flour
1 teaspoon salt
1/4 cup Calvados or Applejack

Mince liver, heart and kidneys; sauté in butter, adding onion as color changes. Shake cream, flour and salt together in a small jar until the lumps disappear; slowly add to the giblets, stirring constantly. Simmer 5 minutes. Season to taste. Add the spirit just before serving.

Try an orange- or apple-flavored spirit in mashed sweet potatoes.

Fruit—Pits and Pulp

FOURTH OF JULY CHICKEN
Worthy of celebration

1 medium cucumber
1 cup sour cream
1/4 teaspoon fresh dill
1/4 cup Applejack
3 slices thick bacon, diced
1 medium onion, diced
1 3-pound fryer chicken, cut into serving pieces
1/4 cup all-purpose flour
1 teaspoon salt
1/4 teaspoon freshly ground pepper

Peel and dice cucumber. Stir together sour cream, dill and Applejack; combine with cucumbers and let stand for 1 hour. In a large pan sauté bacon and onion together. Remove bacon and onion from pan and set aside. Dredge chicken with flour and brown in bacon fat. Drain browned chicken, sprinkle with salt and pepper and place in a baking dish. Combine cucumber mixture with bacon and onions and cover chicken with mixture. Cover dish tightly and bake at 350° for 1 hour. (If you don't want to use your oven, the dish can be cooked on top of the stove or in an electric frypan for 30 minutes. Stir occasionally.)
Serves 4

HAM-APPLE PANCAKE WITH CALVADOS
One crisp 9-inch cake

1/4 pound ham, cubed
1 tablespoon butter
1 large cooking apple, cored, peeled and
    thinly sliced
2 eggs
3/4 cup milk
1 tablespoon Calvados
3/4 cup sifted all-purpose flour
1/2 teaspoon salt

In a 9-inch ovenproof skillet slowly brown ham in butter. Remove ham to drain and cool. Cover the bottom of the pan with apple slices. Sauté gently, turning slices once and adding more butter if necessary. Meanwhile beat eggs and then beat in milk; stir in Calvados. Combine flour and salt and beat into egg mixture until smooth and free of lumps. Stir in ham cubes and pour batter over sautéed apples. Bake in preheated 450° oven 10 to 15 minutes, until pancake puffs up. Reduce temperature to 300° and bake 10 minutes longer. Turn apple-side-up onto plate and serve in wedges.
Serves 2 generously

Apricot

Apricot would win a lot of votes in any "choose-your-favorite-flavor poll," including mine. It is like orange in that it enhances almost any fruit it is combined with—and a lot of other foods as well. It is wonderful with ham, pork, game or fowl. Another excellent use for any of the apricot flavors is on grapefruit, sectioned and left to stand a bit before serving or before broiling.

The majority of apricot liqueurs are made by steeping ripe apricots with grape Brandy and then adding some of the kernel extracts or an apricot eau de vie to round it off.

Abricotine and *Apry* are sweetened French apricot Brandies, while *Barack Palinka* is the Hungarian apricot eau de vie. Mexico produces a red apricot liqueur, *Licor de Chabacano*.

75

Fruit—Pits and Pulp

CANDIED CITRUS PEEL
Choose liqueurs to enhance the fruit flavors

Orange:
6 oranges
2 cups granulated sugar
1 cup water
1 tablespoon or more apricot- or orange-
   flavored liqueur

Grapefruit:
3 grapefruit
2 cups granulated sugar
1 cup water
1 tablespoon Galliano or yellow Chartreuse

Score peel on the fruit in 4 lengthwise sections with point of a knife. Loosen peel from pulp with fingers, removing each section intact. Cut peel into 1/4-inch vertical strips. Trim away most of the pulp remaining on peel with the tip of a knife. Place peel strips in a saucepan (keep them separate if you are making both) and cover with cold water. Bring to boil and cook for 20 minutes. Drain. Repeat process twice with fresh cold water each time. Test for tenderness with a toothpick and if not yet tender continue last cooking period until rind is easily pierced with a toothpick. Drain thoroughly. Combine sugar, 1 cup water and liqueur in a saucepan, stirring to dissolve sugar. Bring to a boil and add peel. Cook over low heat until peel has a clear, candied appearance and syrup is very thick. Remove peel, a few pieces at a time, allowing excess syrup to drain back into pan. Roll strips in granulated sugar. Cool on racks and store in open containers in a dry place. The peels will keep at least a month.
Makes about a pound of each

STRAWSTACK CARROTS
A trick for serving crisp-cooked vegetables;
also good for peas, beans, zucchini,
rutabagas, parsnips or celery root

2 carrots, peeled and cut julienne
1 tablespoon butter
1 teaspoon apricot- or orange-flavored liqueur

Cook vegetables until *barely* tender. Then plunge them into cold water to completely stop the cooking. Drain well, cover and set aside. Just before serving gently warm them in butter with the liqueur, being careful not to overcook.
Serves 2 to 3

𝕭anana

Sweet and often colored yellow, *Crème de Banane* is made by smashing ripe bananas in pure alcohol. There is a strong banana bouquet that is supposed to be particularly popular in Australia. The banana flavor goes well with almost any other fruit. Banana cakes, cookies, breads and pies are all delightfully reinforced by the aftertaste of the liqueur. But be careful, as too much makes the food taste much the same as old-fashioned model airplane glue smells.

Fruit—Pits and Pulp

HOT PEACH LADYFINGER SOUFFLÉ
Peach slices and ladyfingers nestle under
a cap of ground almonds

butter and sugar
2 eggs, separated
5 tablespoons granulated sugar
1/4 cup all-purpose flour
1 cup milk, scalded
2 tablespoons banana- or pineapple-flavored liqueur
1/2 teaspoon vanilla extract or any almond liqueur
3 ladyfingers, split
1 peach, peeled and sliced or 1 10-ounce package
   of frozen peach slices, thawed and drained
1/4 cup ground almonds
1 teaspoon sugar
Fresh Cherry Sauce, following

Butter and sugar a 1-quart soufflé dish; fit with a buttered paper collar. Preheat oven to 375°. With an electric mixer at medium speed beat egg yolks with 5 tablespoons sugar until the mixture falls in ribbons when the beaters are lifted. Then at slow speed gradually beat in flour. Still at slow speed slowly pour in the scalded milk. Transfer mixture to a saucepan and cook over low heat to thicken the custard. Let cool.

Beat egg whites until stiff; add banana or pineapple liqueur and vanilla extract or almond liqueur. Fold egg white mixture into cooled custard. Pour half of soufflé mixture into prepared soufflé dish. Lay the ladyfingers over the mixture and top with peach slices. Pour in remaining soufflé mixture and sprinkle with combined almonds and sugar. Bake in the middle of the oven for 35 to 40 minutes, or until golden and well-puffed. Remove collar and serve hot with Fresh Cherry Sauce.
Serves 2 to 3

FRESH CHERRY SAUCE
Good on custards, cheesecake, ice cream

1/2 cup water
2 tablespoons granulated sugar
1/2 thin lemon slice
1 cup fresh cherries, halved and pitted
1/4 cup currant jelly
Maraschino liqueur, Cherry Heering or
   Kirsch, to taste

Combine water, sugar and lemon in a saucepan and simmer 5 minutes. Add cherries and simmer 10 minutes more. Stir in jelly to melt. Remove from heat and discard lemon. Stir in liqueur.
Makes 1-1/3 cups

𝔅lackberry

Blackberry Brandy was a favorite frontier cure for most ills, particularly diarrhea. Its medicinal reputation may have been used as a license for drinking a bit more of it than necessary, though there are people who still swear by it as a cure-all. The type sold in the United States is very sweet and goes well in dishes made with blueberries and blackberries, though it will color the batter if you use a brand which is dark.

Jerzynowka is a famous Polish blackberry Brandy and a German spirit *Kroatzbeere* (a cousin of our blackberry) is deep purple, not too sweet and has the wonderful bouquet of the wild blackberry. All of these are interchangeable in the kitchen.

Fruit—Pits and Pulp

BLACKBERRY COUNTRY PUDDING
Coarse, chewy, old-fashioned pudding to be served with sour cream and Blackberry Brandy Sauce

3/4 cup butter or margarine
3/4 cup packed brown sugar
1-1/2 cups all-purpose flour,
   lightly spooned into cup and leveled
1 teaspoon baking soda
1/2 teaspoon salt
2 teaspoons ground cinnamon
1/2 teaspoon ground nutmeg
1/4 teaspoon ground coriander
2 eggs, well beaten
3 tablespoons sour cream
1 cup blackberry preserves or jam
1/2 cup chopped walnuts or pecans
Blackberry Brandy Sauce, following
additional sour cream

Preheat oven to 350°. Butter a 1-quart casserole. Cream butter and brown sugar together. Sift flour, soda, salt and spices together. Combine eggs with sour cream; add to butter mixture alternately with dry ingredients. Blend only until ingredients are well combined. Fold in jam and nuts. Pour into casserole and bake 45 to 55 minutes, until toothpick inserted in center comes out clean. Serve hot topped with warm Blackberry Brandy Sauce and a dollop of sour cream.
Serves 8

BLACKBERRY BRANDY SAUCE
A nice sauce for any steamed pudding or ice cream

1 cup granulated sugar
1/4 pound butter or margarine
2 eggs, beaten
1 cup heavy cream
2 tablespoons Blackberry Brandy

Combine sugar, butter, eggs and cream in top of double boiler; stir over hot water until thickened. Add Brandy. Serve warm.

BLACKBERRY SHIVERS
Elegant ice cream

2 cups mashed fresh blackberries
1/2 cup granulated sugar
1 teaspoon lemon juice
1 tablespoon Kirsch, Cassis or
   Blackberry Brandy
1 cup heavy cream, whipped

Combine mashed berries with 1/4 cup of the sugar, lemon juice and liqueur. Beat the remaining 1/4 cup sugar into the whipped cream and fold together with the berry mixture. Freeze in a refrigerator tray until the dessert is firm.
Serves 8

Black Currant/Cassis

The liqueurs made from the black currant are excellent used in steamed puddings and in blackberry or blueberry pie or cobbler. They date back to the 16th century when monks in the Dijon area of France produced a black currant ratafia to which remedial properties were attributed. The potion probably helped mental health, if not physical.

Crème de Cassis is made by macerating the fruit of the black currant in grape Brandy and adding sugar. The result is a sweet, rich, full-flavored liqueur. *Cassis* (less sweet than the crème) has become popular in the United States and Europe as the flavoring agent in the French "Kir," a cocktail made by adding a bit of Cassis or Crème de Cassis to any cold white wine. The name Kir was a cover for a famous French Resistance leader who operated near Dijon during World War II.

In Eastern Europe there is a liqueur made from the black currant called *Bocksbeeren*.

Fruit—Pits and Pulp

CASSIS PEAR PIE
Pears colorfully paired with
Cassis and cherry preserves

pastry for a double-crust pie, see Basics
3/4 cup granulated sugar
1/3 cup all-purpose flour (or more if pears
   are juicy)
grated rind of 1 small orange
1/2 teaspoon ground nutmeg
1/4 teaspoon salt
6 or 7 underripe pears, peeled, cored and sliced
1 tablespoon Cassis or Pear Brandy
1/3 cup cherry preserves
2 tablespoons butter

Prepare 1 recipe Basic Pastry; use half of dough and refrigerate or freeze remainder. Preheat oven to 425°. Line a 9-inch pie pan with pastry. Stir together sugar, flour, orange rind, nutmeg and salt. Combine with pear slices and turn into unbaked pastry shell. Mix Cassis with cherry preserves and spoon over the pears. Dot with butter. Cover with a lattice crust (brush it with cream for extra brownness) and bake 40 minutes.
Serves 6

A-B-C-D PUDDING
A blueberry-cassis delight

2 cups all-purpose flour, spooned lightly
   into cup and leveled
2/3 cup granulated sugar
2 teaspoons baking powder
1/2 teaspoon salt
1 cup blueberries, fresh or frozen
1/2 cup milk
1/2 cup Crème de Cassis
1 egg, well beaten
Lemon Sauce, following
additional blueberries for garnish

In a large bowl stir together with a fork the flour, sugar, baking powder and salt; then stir in the blueberries. Add milk and Cassis to the beaten egg and add this mixture to the dry ingredients; stir just until combined. Spoon into a well-greased and floured 1-quart mold, filling no more than 3/4 full. Cover tightly and steam 1-1/2 hours. Remove from water, set aside the cover and let cool 10 minutes before unmolding. Serve warm with Lemon Sauce; garnish with additional blueberries.
Serves 8 to 10

Note: Pudding may be made ahead and warmed by resteaming in a greased mold for 1 hour.

LEMON SAUCE
It tastes like luscious lemon pie

1 cup granulated sugar
2 tablespoons cornstarch
2 cups water
juice and grated rind of 1 lemon
3 tablespoons butter
2 teaspoons orange-flavored liqueur

Combine sugar and cornstarch in a saucepan; slowly stir in water. Bring to a boil and cook over low heat 8 minutes, stirring constantly. Add lemon juice and rind, butter and liqueur. Stir until butter melts and serve the sauce hot. It can be made ahead and warmed in a double boiler.
Makes 2 cups

BLUEBERRY KIR SAUCE
A winning way to complement almost anything

1 tablespoon butter or margarine
1 tablespoon cornstarch
1/4 cup Cassis
3/4 cup white wine
1 tablespoon lemon juice
1-1/2 cups fresh or 10 ounces frozen blueberries

Melt butter in a saucepan or double boiler. Combine cornstarch and Cassis, eliminating any lumps. Gradually stir into melted butter. Add white wine and lemon juice. Continue to cook over low heat, stirring until thick. Add berries and heat through.
Makes 2-1/2 cups

Baste whole ham or a ham slice frequently with apricot-flavored liqueur during the last portion of the roasting period. Then serve with a sauce made by heating puréed apricot preserves with apricot-flavored Brandy.

Peach and Blackberry Brandies are delicious with fresh fruit and cheese. Try blending the spirit into cream cheese and spreading on slices of fresh fruit for dessert.

Serve washed fresh strawberries with raw sugar and Kirsch, orange- or apricot-flavored liqueur or Fraise. Guests pick up berries by the stem, dip them into the spirit and then into the sugar for a cool, simple and impressive dessert.

Cherry

The cherry eau-de-vie, *Kirsch* or *Kirschwasser,* is considered by many people to be undrinkable. The Swiss often pass the strong, dry spirit together with sugar lumps which the ladies may dip into the Kirsch and then suck (a sort of instant liqueur). This is only semi-successful as it's impossible to come through the experience without sticky fingers and the sugar lumps have a natural tendency to disintegrate when moist. This crumbling action usually takes place when the lump is halfway to the mouth. It all leads to unladylike finger lickin'.

Kirsch is also made in Alsace and in Germany, where it often goes under the name of *Schwarzwalder. Rote Kirsch* is a deep red and bittersweet German Kirsch; *Kirsch Peureaux* is sweet, but not bitter.

Whether you enjoy drinking it or not, Kirsch is valuable in the kitchen, particularly an imported Kirsch. America's version is sweeter and isn't recommended for a Swiss cheese fondue, though it can be used in fruit concoctions. Any fruit takes on glamour when it and Kirsch have been romancing together in the refrigerator for some time before they travel to the table. But do use it sparingly as the flavor is very penetrating.

Cherry Heering, now called *Peter Heering,* is one of the most popular liqueurs sold in the United States, perhaps because the cherry pits present in the distillation keep it from being overly sweet. It is excellent in cooking meats and in baking.

Maraschino originated in a portion of Italy that is now incorporated into Yugoslavia. The liqueur is sweet, clear or tinted red and highly concentrated in flavor. It is distilled from fermented sour maraschino cherries and their crushed kernels—sometimes the distillate is perfumed with flower blossom extracts. It is lovely in fruit salads, jellies, trifles and sorbets.

Cerasella is another fine Italian cherry liqueur, red in color. Its unique, rich flavor comes from herbs gathered in the Abruzzi Mountains.

Grant's Morella Cherry Brandy is made of the famous cherries from Kent, England. It is lighter in texture than most cherry liqueurs.

Cherry Marnier, Rocher and *Guignolet* are some of the light French cherry liqueurs. *Cherry and Brandy* is a similar liqueur while *Crème de Black Cherry* is sweeter.

Vishnoyovayá Nalivka is a Russian cherry liqueur and *Wishniak* is a cherry liqueur from Israel. *Cherry Blossom Liqueur* comes from Japan.

All can be used in cherry breads, cobblers, pies, tarts, bars or desserts. Any cherry sauce or filling is improved with a few dashes from the bottle but use much less of those with bitter undertones. They are excellent, however, with duckling, pork and ham.

GLACÉ FOR STUFFED DRIED FRUITS
Can also be used on fresh fruits

2 cups granulated sugar
1 cup water
1/4 cup cream of tartar
1/4 teaspoon Kirsch

Stir the sugar, water and cream of tartar together in a saucepan until sugar is dissolved; cook over medium heat without stirring until mixture turns pale yellow and reaches the hard crack stage (about 300°). Remove from heat and add Kirsch. Plunge the saucepan into very cold water to check the boiling; then place in hot water to keep the syrup from hardening. Begin dipping in the fruits, or spoon the syrup over them on a rack.

Fruit suggestions for glacéing: prunes stuffed with walnuts, dates stuffed with almonds, fresh tangerine sections, strawberries (not hulled), stemmed cherries, any dried fruit stuffed with Smooth Fondant (see page 117).

CHERRY BRANDY SHERBET
Fresh red cherries and Brandy flavor
a refreshing, low-cal dessert

1-1/2 cups granulated sugar
2-1/2 cups water
3 cups fresh, pitted red cherries
2 tablespoons cherry-flavored Brandy,
    Maraschino liqueur or Kirsch

Combine sugar and 1-1/2 cups water in a saucepan; boil 5 minutes and cool. In another saucepan combine remaining 1 cup water with pitted cherries. Cook over medium heat just long enough to soften cherries. Pour cherries with their cooking liquid into a blender and purée or press them through a sieve. Mix together the sugar syrup and the cherry purée. Stir in Brandy or liqueur and pour into can of a churn-type freezer. Turn until sherbet is of proper consistency. Remove dasher, plug hole in can top and leave tub in ice, or place in freezer, to ripen for an hour or longer.
Makes 1/2 gallon

RED BERRY SAUCE
Try this with poached fruit,
fresh strawberries or on waffles

1 cup sliced fresh strawberries
1 cup fresh raspberries
1/4 cup granulated sugar
2 tablespoons lemon juice
Kirsch, Framboise, Fraise or orange-flavored
    liqueur, to taste

Combine all ingredients in a blender and purée; strain.
Makes 1-1/2 cups

Cranberry

Cranberry Cordial has been introduced to the United States by a French firm and the sweet-tart flavor has proven to be very popular. It is a welcome addition to cranberry breads, muffins, desserts, salads and it can add a special touch to your favorite turkey sauce.

CRANBERRY CHUTNEY
Excellent with turkey, ham, goose or game

1 thin-skinned orange, thinly sliced
   with the skin on and seeded
4 cups (1 pound) cranberries
1 apple, peeled, cored and diced
1 cup raw sugar or packed brown sugar
1/2 cup or more finely cut preserved ginger
1/2 cup chopped mixed candied fruit
3/4 cup cider vinegar
1/4 cup orange-flavored liqueur
1/4 cup cranberry-flavored liqueur or dry red wine

5 whole cloves
5 whole allspice
1 teaspoon salt
1 tablespoon mustard seeds

Chop orange slices into small bits. Combine all ingredients in a large kettle, bring to a boil and simmer 20 to 25 minutes, or until thickened. Stir occasionally, particularly after the first 15 minutes. Spoon into sterilized jars and seal. Store in refrigerator or cupboard. Serve cold.
Makes 1 quart

Peach

To obtain the best flavor, extracts of the peach kernel must be added to peach-impregnated Brandy. The peach spirits are good in any dish already containing peaches. Sprinkle a little on the peach slices for a pie or flavor the whipped cream served with it. Flavor the batter and the filling of a cake, use one in peach cobbler or sprinkle some over fresh or frozen peaches and berries for a compote. They are interesting, too, in sauces for ham, ham loaf and brushed over a ham slice before baking.

Southern Comfort is a whiskey liqueur made in the United States from a Bourbon base, flavored with fresh peaches and oranges. It, too, is delightful in cooking—especially puddings, pies and ducks (either wild or domestic).

NUT LOGS
Can be shaped as individual candies
or formed into larger rolls for slicing

1 7-1/2-ounce jar marshmallow cream
1 tablespoon Southern Comfort, Brandy or Rum
1 teaspoon vanilla extract
yellow food coloring (optional)
3-1/2 cups (1 pound) confectioners' sugar
1 pound caramels
2 to 3 cups coarsely chopped nuts

Combine first 5 ingredients, kneading in the last of the sugar. Form into rolls and wrap in waxed paper. Place in freezer until a very hard candy is formed. Melt caramels in top of a double boiler. Remove from heat but keep over hot water. Spread about 2 inches of candy with caramel and press nuts firmly into caramel with hands. Continue with caramel and nuts until rolls are completely covered. Cool. Wrap and store in a cool, dry place.
Makes about 5 pounds

Pineapple/Ananas

The pineapple liqueurs, *Pineapple-flavored Brandy* and *Crème d'Ananas,* are often based upon Rum and matured in wooden casks which give them a very special flavor. Hawaii is our principle source. They are natural flavor-mates of chocolate and of almost any other fruit. Excellent when used to echo the pineapple flavor in fruit salads, compotes, pies and candy.

PINEAPPLE PANCAKE

A giant crêpe which can hold any kind of fresh or prepared fruit; serve it for brunch or as an unusual dessert

Pancake:
1 egg, beaten
2 tablespoons granulated sugar
pinch salt
2-1/2 tablespoons all-purpose flour
1/4 cup milk
1 teaspoon pineapple-, peach- or orange-flavored liqueur
1 tablespoon butter

Pineapple Filling:
1/2 cup juice drained from canned pineapple (if fresh pineapple is used, substitute orange or pineapple juice)
1 teaspoon cornstarch
1 tablespoon butter or margarine
1/2 cup crushed or chopped pineapple, fresh or canned
1 teaspoon pineapple- or orange-flavored liqueur

Pancake: In the order listed, measure pancake ingredients except butter into a jar, cover tightly and shake until just blended. Melt butter in a heavy 8- to 10-inch ovenproof skillet. Pour batter into skillet and place in cold oven. Set oven to 550° and bake until pancake is puffy and cooked throughout, about 20 minutes. Slide out onto a platter, fill and fold 2 sides over center. Serve hot.

Pineapple Filling: In a saucepan stir cold juice into cornstarch. Add butter, fruit and spirit. Stirring constantly, bring to simmering over medium heat and cook 5 minutes.
Serves 2

Note: The pancakes may be made ahead, folded in thirds and wrapped in foil to store in the freezer. To serve, heat in 500° oven for 10 minutes.

Plum/Prune

Crème de Prunelle is sweet, of course, while *Prunelle, Quetsch* and *Mirabelle* are eaux de vie. *Slivovitz* is a true plum Brandy in that it is distilled (in fact it undergoes double distillation) from plums. However, unlike an eau de vie, the fiery brew is aged for a year in casks. It then has fresh blue plums added to it for extra flavor; it is not sweetened. After bottling it is usually allowed to mature five years before shipping. Yugoslavia is the major producer, but her neighbors brew the beverage, too. All are plum delightful in plum pie, plum pudding, prune whip, prune bread or almost any combination of fruits.

PLUM GOOD BREAD PUDDING
Prunes and Prunelle or Quetsch
lift this out of the ordinary

2 eggs
3/4 cup milk
1/4 cup granulated or raw sugar
2 tablespoons Prunelle or Quetsch
1/4 teaspoon ground cinnamon
1/4 teaspoon salt
1/3 to 1/2 cup chopped prunes or raisins
3 slices bread, torn
Prunelle Sauce, following

Preheat oven to 350° and butter a small soufflé dish or individual baking dishes. Beat together eggs, milk, sugar, liqueur, cinnamon and salt. Stir in dried fruit and bread; pour into buttered dish and bake 1 hour. Serve with Prunelle Sauce while pudding is still puffed up and proud.
Serves 3 to 4

PRUNELLE SAUCE
Marvelous over bread pudding, fruitcake,
raisin pie, mince or apple pie. Made with other
liqueurs it can be used for other desserts

1/2 cup granulated sugar
1 tablespoon cornstarch
1/4 teaspoon salt
1 cup water
2 tablespoons butter
1 tablespoon Prunelle or Quetsch, or to taste
1/8 teaspoon grated nutmeg

Stir together sugar, cornstarch and salt; add water and bring to a boil, stirring regularly to prevent lumps. Simmer about 5 minutes; then add butter, liqueur and nutmeg (freshly grated is nicest if you have a nutmeg grater and good knuckles, but the other will do).
Makes about 1 cup

Raspberry/Framboise

Raspberry liqueurs— *Crème de Framboise, Framboise Sauvage*—are made in France and Holland. They are sweet and much different than the French eau de vie, called simply *Framboise. Raspberry-flavored Brandy* is made in the United States and is similar to the European liqueurs. All are excellent in any fruit dish, compote, pie, fruit salad, gelatin dish or in any dish containing raspberries, peaches or strawberries.

RASPBERRY PUDDING MOLD
Quick to make, but it must spend
a night in the refrigerator

15 to 16 slices white bread (1 12-ounce loaf)
4 cups fresh raspberries or 3 10-ounce packages
    frozen berries, thawed but not drained
1-1/2 cups granulated sugar (only 1/2 cup if
    frozen berries are used)
1 tablespoon Framboise or orange-flavored liqueur
3/4 cup heavy cream, whipped
sugar
Framboise, chocolate- or orange-flavored liqueur

Leave slices of bread uncovered in a warm place for several hours so the texture becomes firm. Remove crusts from bread. Bring berries, sugar and the tablespoon of liqueur to a boil and simmer 3 minutes (5 if fresh berries are used), stirring to dissolve the sugar.

Spoon some of the syrup into a bowl. Dip bread into remaining purée, coating both sides, and arrange the slices to cover bottom and overlap on sides of bowl. Fill center with more slices of bread which have been coated on both sides with purée, spooning purée between layers. Pour any remaining purée over the last layer of bread. Set a plate with a 2-pound weight on top (heavy pewter plates work well). Set the bowl on yet another plate to catch any drips, and chill overnight or up to 36 hours.

Shortly before serving, loosen the edges of the pudding with a small, sharp knife. Turn out onto a serving dish and bedeck with whipped cream which has been flavored to taste with sugar and a complementary spirit.
Serves 8

MELBA SAUCE
Puréed raspberries with Framboise

2 10-ounce packages frozen raspberries
1 cup currant, or any tart, jelly
1 cup granulated sugar
1/4 cup water
4 teaspoons Framboise
1 teaspoon cornstarch
1 teaspoon fresh lemon juice

Combine in a saucepan the raspberries with their juice, jelly, sugar and water; bring to a boil. Stir Framboise and cornstarch together until smooth, then combine with the hot raspberry mixture. Stir in lemon juice. Continue cooking and stirring over medium heat until thick and clear, about 5 minutes. Strain to remove seeds and pour either into hot, sterilized jars with self-sealing lids or into covered containers to refrigerate. Serve heated.
Makes about 2 cups

Sloe Gin

Sloe Gin is a deep red liqueur made by steeping ripe sloe berries (the fruit of the British blackthorn bush and a relative of the plum) in Gin. Other fruits may occasionally be added to increase the flavor. The liqueur is matured in wood and is good for the digestion. Even gall bladder sufferers, who find other spirits an anathema, are often able to tolerate it. The liqueur is interesting in fruit cobblers, pies, etc.

BUTTER FOR FRUIT BREADS
Lovely, too, on waffles or pancakes

1/4 pound very soft butter or margarine
1 tablespoon honey
1/4 teaspoon grated lemon peel

1/8 teaspoon grated orange peel
1/4 cup (2 ounces) Sloe Gin, Galliano or Strega

Whip all ingredients together until light and fluffy. Serve on anything that likes a sweet topping.
Makes 1/2 cup

𝔖𝔱𝔯𝔞𝔴𝔟𝔢𝔯𝔯𝔶/𝔉𝔯𝔞𝔦𝔰𝔢

Fraise is an eau de vie. When you note *Strawberry Liqueur*, *Strawberry-flavored Brandy* or *Crème de Fraise* on the label you know the contents is sweet. All are delicious in any dish where strawberries are used or would be welcome, and they are almost always interchangeable with their raspberry counterparts.

WILD STRAWBERRY/FRAISE DE BOIS
Fraise de Bois is made from France's tiny wild strawberries and can be used interchangeably with either the strawberry- or raspberry-flavored liqueurs. If you have either of the latter on hand, use them instead and save the wild strawberry liqueur to savor in a glass as the special treat that it is.

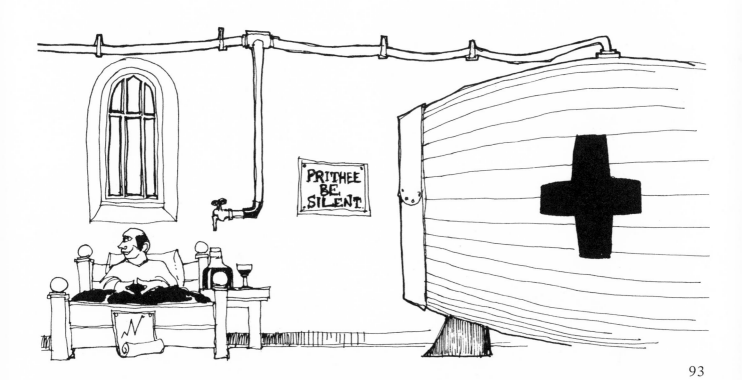

SHINY STRAWBERRY PIE
Whole berries with a beautiful glaze

pastry for a single-crust pie, see Basics
1 cup granulated sugar
3 tablespoons cornstarch
1 tablespoon strawberry-, raspberry- or orange-
  flavored liqueur
water
red food coloring
1 pint or more whole strawberries, hulled
1 cup heavy cream (optional)
candied mint or fresh mint sprigs (optional)

Preheat oven to 425°. Prepare 1 recipe Basic Pastry
and use 1/4 of dough for shell; refrigerate or freeze
remainder. Roll out dough as directed in recipe and
line an 8- or 9-inch pie pan. Pierce shell with tines of
fork and bake at 425° for 10 to 12 minutes. Cool.

Stir sugar and cornstarch together in a saucepan. Measure liqueur into a 1-cup measure; fill with
water to make 1 cup. Gradually stir liqueur-water
into sugar mixture and cook together 5 minutes
over medium heat; stir in a few drops red food
coloring. Arrange whole berries in pie shell and
pour slightly cooled cornstarch mixture over all.
Chill before serving.

If you wish, serve topped with heavy cream
whipped and flavored with a bit more of the liqueur.
For extra eye appeal garnish with candied mint
leaves or a sprig of fresh mint on each portion.
Serves 6 to 8

FRIED STRAWBERRIES
Bring out the fondue pot and
and let guests cook their own dessert

1 pint large, fresh strawberries
1 cup apricot jam
1/2 to 3/4 cup chopped almonds
2 large eggs
2 teaspoons Fraise or Kirsch
1 cup fine saltine crumbs
peanut oil for deep-frying

Wash berries, hull and drain until completely dry. Force jam through a strainer into a small shallow bowl. In three separate shallow bowls place chopped almonds, eggs whipped with Fraise or Kirsch, and saltine crumbs. Dip berries in jam, then roll them in almonds. Quickly dip almond-coated berries in beaten eggs and roll in crumbs. Place in a single layer on a large plate and refrigerate for several hours.

Just before serving fill a saucepan or fondue pot with oil to a depth of 3 inches and heat oil to 360°. Fry berries, a few at a time, until golden brown. Remove from heat and drain on paper towels. Serve warm.
Serves 6 to 8

STRAWBERRY ZIGGURAT
A sparkling pyramid of strawberries

1 10-ounce package frozen raspberries or 1 cup
   fresh berries plus 1/3 cup granulated sugar
2 pints large fresh strawberries, hulled
Fraise, Framboise, Kirsch or an orange-
   flavored liqueur
pistachio nuts
1 cup heavy cream

Purée the raspberries in a blender; strain to remove seeds. Dip each strawberry into the spirit of your choice and arrange them pyramid fashion in a serving dish. When the pyramid is "topped out," spoon raspberry purée over to coat the berries. Sprinkle the shiny mound with pistachios and serve with a bowl of cream whipped with sugar and gently flavored with spirit.
Serves 8

GOLD & SILVER

Gold and Silver Flakes

Don't Eat Them, Drink Them!

YES, TRULY, real flakes of gold and silver were originally added to herb-blend liqueurs flavored with aniseed and caraway as treatment for, or prevention of, certain dread diseases. In India in the establishments of men of wealth, gold dust used to be sprinkled over the pudding or sweet course at any meal where an important guest was being honored. This was done for two reasons: to protect the health of the guest (probably an extra precaution as sanitation was none too good) and to honor him. Real gold and silver leaf are still used as decoration on food in India and on chocolate candies and petit fours in Europe.

So the German liqueur, *Danziger Goldwasser,* first made commercially in 1598, is still shipped in great quantities to India (and elsewhere) using the original Danzig formula. *Danziger Silverwasser* is said to have exactly the same flavor base, but with silver flakes afloat in it rather than gold. For some reason the silver is not quite as palatable as the gold.

The Garnier Company has been producing a French "goldwater" called *Liqueur d'Or* since 1890. It is pale yellow in color with gold flakes shimmering in the golden bath. Several other liqueur makers now distribute a colorless liqueur containing gold flakes.

In all of these liqueurs, the flakes of gold or silver rest at the bottom and go into suspension when you tip the bottle—just as when you shake a paperweight to evoke a snowstorm, you temporarily suspend the snow. There is even one with a wind-up ballerina inside. She will dance on cue in a shower of golden snowflakes. These bottles all make such lovely adult toys that it is almost a shame to drink the liqueur and even more of a shame to cook with it. Why not use a less expensive caraway- or anise-flavored liqueur to cook with and save the gold to sip when honoring guests?

97

Herbs & Spices

Herbs, Spices and Blends

When No Single Flavor Predominates, It's an "Herb Blend"

SPICE AND HERB blends are excellent in cooking vegetables and in meat dishes. Here it's a matter of following your nose from bottle to bottle, just as you do when you're reaching for a pinch of something or other from your herb shelf. Only in the herb liqueurs do you have as many as 130 different leaves, roots, barks or seeds blended for a pleasant flavor. It's simpler to add a drop or two than 130 pinches!

Most herb-blend liqueurs are somewhat interchangeable in recipes. The sweeter are best used in desserts, with fruits and to flavor sweet vegetables such as peas, corn, carrots and squash. Those with bitter undertones must be used carefully but are interesting additions in soups, stews, bean dishes and with spicy food mixtures. All of them are useful in the kitchen, providing you approach them nose first and tip the bottle with a light hand.

Chartreuse, which dates back to the 16th century, is a much-imitated herb liqueur. Its formula is so complicated that it took 30 years for the Carthusian monks to make the first "health liqueur" from the original recipe bequeathed them by a French alchemist. By 1735 they were blending the 130 rare aromatic herbs with a base of fine Brandy to produce *Elixir Végétal* (136° proof). Later they developed two additional products: *Green Chartreuse,* which is sweeter and lower in proof than the original (about 110° proof) and, a still mellower and more delicate, *Yellow Chartreuse* (86° proof).

The "D.O.M." found on each *Benedictine* bottle stands for the Latin Deo Optimo Maximo (To God, most Good, most Great). A Benedictine monk is said to have evolved the elixir primarily to combat the malaria which was prevalent in the early 1500's, but also to revive the tired monks (who doubtless needed it, as the Benedictine rule was a strict one and allowed only a few hours sleep each night). Benedictine became popular medicine and in 1534 Francis I, King of France, is said to have praised its virtues. During the French Revolution the Abbey was destroyed and the Benedictines dispersed. Seventy years later the recipe for *Benedictine, ad majorem Dei Gloriam* (Benedictine, for the greater Glory of God) came into the hands of a descendant of the procureur fiscal for the abbey. He was a wine merchant as well and eventually established a vast business based upon the old recipe. Although the product is no longer made by a religious order, the D.O.M. is still on the bottles.

Benedictine and Brandy (B and B) is drier than plain Benedictine and is very popular in the United States and Canada. It began as a combination that people mixed at home to sweeten Brandy and make it more palatable after dinner. It is now bottled as a separate product and is useful where a more subtle herb flavor would be interesting, as in soufflés, veal dishes, etc.

Herbs, Spices and Blends

Galliano is a soft, sweet Italian herb liqueur with a great deal of angelica flavor. It comes to market in a distinctive, tall bottle. The liqueur is named after Major Guiseppe Galliano who was instrumental in ending the Italian-Abyssinian War of 1895-96. An unusual memorial, but more lasting than most. See the chapter on Angelica.

Watch out for *Strega*. According to legend when two people taste this pale yellow liqueur together they are forever united. It must be the 70 Italian barks and herbs in the formula. Here again, angelica seems to be a major flavor contributor.

La Senacole is made by the monks of the Abbey of Senanque, founded by the Cistercian Order in 1148. The liqueur is made from the aromatic plants growing on the stony hillsides around the Abbey and is named after the river that flows through the valley below. The secret formula is still held by the prior of Senanque and the herbs are still prepared by the faithful fathers.

Izarra ("Star," in the Basque language) is an herb liqueur also produced in two variations distinguished by colors, one yellow and one green. The base is Armagnac which is flavored with herbs grown in the French Pyrénées. *Trappistine* is also based upon Armagnac, though in this liqueur the herbs come from the Doubs Mountains. *Raspail* is mentioned under Angelica, its major ingredient. *Aiguebelle* is a Trappist formula based upon more than 50 French herbs. It, too, appears in two varieties, yellow and green.

Elixir d'Anvers is the Belgian national liqueur. It is different from the others in that it is soft but not too sweet. There is a somewhat bittersweet taste.

There is nothing soft about *Cynar*, the Italian liqueur made from artichokes and herbs. It is definitely an acquired taste.

Ginger-flavored Brandy is popular in England, Holland and the United States. It has a distinctly gingery taste and smell and can be used to impart a hint of ginger to whatever you are baking. The liqueur seems to combine particularly well with orange.

Crème de Vanille tastes just as vanilla extract smells but doesn't taste. Like vanilla extract, it enhances almost any dessert.

Jagermeister is a dark German herb liqueur. It is very strong and is another acquired taste. Approach it cautiously in the kitchen. *Echt Stonsdorfer,* another German herb favorite, has a distinctly fruity flavor derived from bilberries.

Monte Aguila is a Jamaican liqueur with pimento (allspice) as the principal flavor. There are several liqueurs similar to Aguila and all are slightly bitter, quite spicy and pleasant with meats and some vegetables. *Piment-O-Dram* has the added spice of red pepper in its formula and *Pimento Liqueur* is another spicy specialty of the Caribbean.

St. Hallvard is a Norwegian liqueur based upon potato spirits and flavored with herbs. *Tapio* is a neighborly Finnish product flavored with juniper berries and herbs. Try these with fish.

ASPARAGUS QUICHE
A winning flavor combination

Crust:
pastry for single-crust pie, see Basics
1/4 to 1/2 teaspoon cayenne
1 tablespoon soft butter

Filling:
1/2 cup shredded Swiss cheese
1/2 cup chopped cooked ham (optional)
1 cup chopped, cooked asparagus, plus
   6 cooked asparagus spears (fresh or frozen)
1 teaspoon salt
1/2 teaspoon freshly ground pepper
pinch of ground nutmeg
pinch of cayenne
1 tablespoon Piment-O-Dram or dark Rum
4 eggs
2 cups heavy cream

Crust: Preheat oven to 425°. Prepare 1 recipe Basic Pastry; set aside 1/4 of dough (about 1 cup) for quiche crust and refrigerate or freeze remainder. Combine 1 cup pastry mixture with cayenne. Roll on lightly floured surface and line a 9-inch pan. Butter inside of crust.

Filling: Sprinkle bottom of shell with shredded cheese and ham (if used). Cook asparagus as desired or according to package directions. Select 6 slender spears to serve as garnish and chop the remainder. Place chopped asparagus in blender together with seasonings, liqueur and eggs; purée. Combine the purée with cream and pour over the cheese. Arrange the asparagus spears in a pattern radiating from the center of the quiche. Bake 15 minutes. Reduce heat to 300° and bake 40 minutes longer or until a knife inserted in the center comes out clean.
Serves 6 to 8

Herbs, Spices and Blends

CHICKEN CURRY QUICHE
Ginger, chili and curry hint of the Middle East

Crust:
pastry for a single-crust pie, see Basics
1/4 teaspoon Indian curry powder
1 tablespoon soft butter

Filling:
1-1/2 cups diced cooked chicken or turkey
1/2 cup grated Swiss cheese
4 eggs
2 cups heavy cream
1/2 teaspoon salt
1/2 teaspoon Indian curry powder
1/4 teaspoon chili powder
1/8 teaspoon ground pepper
1 teaspoon ginger-flavored Brandy

Crust: Preheat oven to 425°. Prepare 1 recipe Basic
Pastry; set aside 1/4 of dough (about 1 cup) for
quiche crust and refrigerate or freeze remainder.
Combine 1 cup pastry dough with curry powder;
proceed as directed in Basic Pastry recipe. Spread
unbaked shell with butter.
Filling: Distribute chicken and cheese over bottom
of pastry. Beat eggs and combine with heavy cream
and seasonings. Stir in ginger Brandy. Pour over
chicken and cheese; bake 15 minutes. Reduce oven
temperature to 325° and bake 40 minutes longer or
until a knife inserted in center comes out clean.
Serves 6 to 8

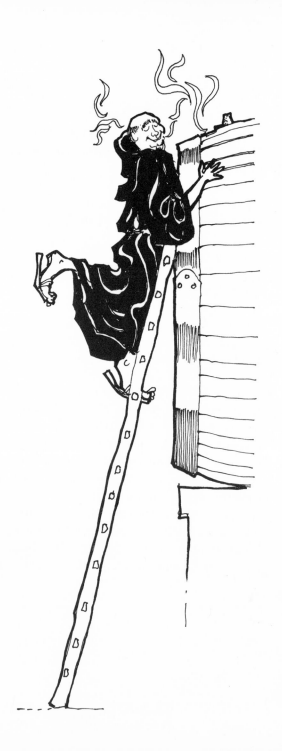

STUFFED PATTYPAN WITH CHARTREUSE
*Multiply recipe by the number of persons
to be served*

1 pattypan (summer) squash
1 teaspoon finely chopped shallot
1 teaspoon butter
1/4 cup finely torn bread
pinch salt
freshly ground pepper
1/4 teaspoon yellow Chartreuse
2 teaspoons dried bread crumbs
1 teaspoon butter
1 teaspoon grated Cheddar cheese

Cook unpeeled squash in boiling, salted water just until tender; cool. Cut a thin slice off the top of squash and scoop out the inside with a teaspoon, leaving 1/4-inch thick shell. Finely chop pulp including seeds and top. Sauté shallot in butter and combine with squash pulp, bread, seasonings and Chartreuse; spoon into shell.

Brown dried bread crumbs in butter, combine with grated cheese and sprinkle over the filling. Bake in preheated 350° oven 20 minutes or until cheese melts and crumbs sizzle.

GINGER-GLAZED CHICKEN OR TURKEY WINGS
The glaze is also good on spareribs, hamburger or ham

1/4 cup soy sauce
2 tablespoons honey
1/2 cup ginger-flavored Brandy
1-1/2 tablespoons fresh lemon juice
1/2 cup chicken stock or bouillon
1 clove garlic, minced
3 pounds chicken or turkey wings,
   or baby spareribs

Combine soy sauce, honey, Brandy, lemon juice, stock and garlic to make a marinade. Add the poultry or meat, making certain it is all covered. Marinate 2 to 3 hours or longer.

Preheat oven to 350°. Place the wings or ribs on a rack in a shallow baking pan, pour the marinade over the pieces, cover with foil and bake for 30 minutes. Remove the foil, baste, turn and continue cooking for another 15 to 30 minutes, basting frequently, until the meat is tender and nicely browned.
Serves 4 to 6

ITALIAN SAUSAGE BREAD
Pretzel-shaped loaves hold spicy sausage

1-1/2 pounds sweet Italian sausage
   (about 8 fat links)
about 3 cups milk
3 tablespoons any herb-flavored Italian liqueur
6 cups unsifted all-purpose flour
2 packages dry yeast
1 tablespoon salt
2 teaspoons Italian herb seasoning
1 egg yolk
1 tablespoon cold water

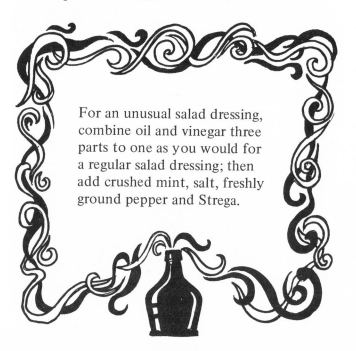

For an unusual salad dressing, combine oil and vinegar three parts to one as you would for a regular salad dressing; then add crushed mint, salt, freshly ground pepper and Strega.

Remove casings from sausages and flatten each link to about 1/4-inch thickness. Sauté patties slowly to render out fat, trying not to make the meat crusty. Drain fat into a 2-cup measure; add milk and liqueur to make 2 cups. Pour milk mixture into saucepan and heat until bubbles begin to form around the edge of the pan. Remove from heat. Meanwhile, combine 3 cups of the flour with dry yeast and salt in a large mixing bowl. Add 1 cup cold milk to the hot milk mixture and pour into the flour in the bowl. Stir to combine well and add enough additional flour to make a soft dough. Turn onto floured surface and knead 10 minutes until smooth and elastic.

Divide dough in half and roll each half to make a rectangle about 18 inches long and 8 inches wide. Cut sausage into 1/2-inch strips and lay onto rolled dough in 3 rows parallel to the longest edge; sprinkle dough with Italian seasoning. Turn long side of dough over meat and roll tightly as for cinnamon rolls. Place long rolls of dough on greased baking sheets and arrange each in a pretzel shape. Brush breads with salad oil and let rise in a warm place for 1 hour or until a slight indentation remains when dough is pressed with a finger. Brush loaves with a mixture of egg yolk and water. Bake in preheated 425° oven 45 minutes or until browned and cooked through. Keeps about 1 week.
Makes 2 large loaves

ROAST TURKEY WITH VEGETABLE STUFFING
A colorful change from regular bread stuffing

1 12- to 14-pound turkey
2 small eggs or 1 large egg
2 to 4 tablespoons Piment-O-Dram, green
　Chartreuse, Cognac or Bourbon
3 cups fresh corn, or 1 16-ounce can each cream-
　style corn and whole kernel corn
1 medium onion, chopped
1 cup grated raw carrot or sweet potato
1/4 cup finely diced green pepper
6 cups small bread cubes, toasted
1 tablespoon seasoning salt, see Basics
1/2 teaspoon coarsely ground pepper
1/2 teaspoon poultry seasoning
1/2 teaspoon salt

Beat egg and spirit together in a large bowl. Combine with other ingredients in order listed. If the mixture seems too dry, add a little white wine or stock. Stuff loosely into the turkey; fasten cavities closed. Place bird in a cold oven and set thermostat to 450°; roast 30 minutes. Then reduce heat to 325° and bake for about 3 hours or to an internal temperature of 185° on a meat thermometer. Baste occasionally while roasting. For extra flavor, bird may be brushed with a mixture in equal proportions of melted butter and dry Vermouth.
Serves 16 to 20

SOUR CREAM CHARTREUSE SAUCE
A sauce for fish, raw vegetables or baked potatoes

1-1/4 cups sour cream
1/8 teaspoon ground ginger
1/2 cup chopped watercress
1/4 to 1/2 teaspoon salt, to taste
1/4 teaspoon green Chartreuse

Stir ingredients together and serve, or whirl in the blender to make a green sauce.
Makes about 1-3/4 cups

Green Chartreuse or Pernod will make an excellent dressing for tossed salad with a little freshly squeezed lemon juice.

Alcohol helps tenderize meats.

CROWN ROAST OF LAMB WITH SWEETBREADS IN CHARTREUSE SAUCE

*Sweetbreads rest regally
in the center of a crown roast*

Roast:
12-rib crown roast of lamb
2 garlic cloves
coarse salt
cracked pepper
1 tablespoon green Chartreuse
1 cup fruity white wine (not sweet)

Sweetbreads:
2 pair sweetbreads (not more than 24 hours old)
2 teaspoons vinegar or lemon juice
1 teaspoon salt

Chartreuse Sauce:
4 tablespoons butter or margarine
1 cup sliced fresh mushrooms
4 tablespoons all-purpose flour
1-1/2 cups milk
1/4 cup heavy cream
1 teaspoon salt
freshly ground pepper
1/2 teaspoon seasoning salt, see Basics
1 tablespoon green Chartreuse

Roast: Cover bone tips with foil. Crush garlic and mix with salt, pepper and green Chartreuse. Thoroughly rub surfaces of roast with the mixture. Place roast on a rack in a shallow roasting pan. An hour and a half before serving slip the roast into a preheated 350° oven. Baste every 15 minutes with white wine.

Sweetbreads: Wash and soak sweetbreads in ice water for 1 hour. Drain, place in pot and cover with fresh water; add vinegar or lemon juice and salt. Simmer gently 15 minutes; drain. Cover with cold water and let the sweetbreads cool. Drain again. Remove the membranes, connective tissue and tubes (not a difficult job). Cut into bite-size pieces, cover and keep warm while preparing Chartreuse Sauce. Sweetbreads may also be prepared in advance; refrigerate until ready to use.

Sauce: Melt butter in a large saucepan and gently sauté the mushrooms. Remove mushrooms and set aside. Stir flour into butter to make a roux, taking care not to brown. Slowly stir in milk, cream, salt, pepper and seasoning salt. Stir constantly until mixture thickens and then cook gently over low heat for about 30 minutes, stirring occasionally to prevent scorching (this can be done in a double boiler). Shortly before serving, stir in sweetbreads and mushrooms, and heat through. Just before pouring sweetbreads into the center of the crown roast of lamb, add Chartreuse to taste.

Serves 8 to 10

Note: The sauce may be served without the sweetbreads as an accompaniment to lamb or ham. It can also be served with seafood en casserole.

CHARTREUSE BREAD
Thin, crisp, cracker-like sheets of bread

1 package dry yeast
2 cups warm water
1 teaspoon sugar
2 teaspoons salt
1/4 cup green Chartreuse
5 cups unsifted all-purpose flour

Preheat oven to 350°. Dissolve yeast in 1 cup warm water. Add sugar, salt, remaining water and Chartreuse. Stir in just enough flour to form a soft dough. Turn dough out onto floured board and knead about 4 minutes, until a smooth ball is formed. Cut off approximately 1/8 of the dough, shape into a small ball and roll out as thin as you can. Place the dough on an ungreased 12x14-inch cookie sheet (it will be irregular in shape). Bake 15 minutes or until lightly browned and crisp. Remove from oven and prop the sheet of bread on edge to cool. Follow the same procedure for the other "loaves."
Makes 8 sheets

Mint/Peppermint

Mint Is Marvelous in the Kitchen

MINT IS a flavor of infinite use. Wherever the freshness of mint would be welcome add a few drops of the spirit. It does wonders for many foods: peas, spinach, lamb, pork, any Middle Eastern dish and almost any fruit salad, compote or dessert, particularly those made with pears or chocolate. Try it in chocolate pudding or add it to the topping you use with the pudding. Pour a bit into the batter for a steamed pudding or a chocolate cake, or add to the filling or frosting for the cake.

All that is mint is not green. The makers bottle it in its clear form as well as tinted red, gold or green. Given a choice buy the white or clear for cooking. You can always add a bit of food coloring should you want color.

Different brands of *Crème de Menthe* are flavored from different varieties of mint, grown in different areas. The finest flavoring mints are said to come from England but the green mint liqueur that is possibly the most famous is *Freezomint* made by the French firm of Cusenier. They began making their product at the family home in the Jura Mountains from the mint gathered there. Another popular French mint liqueur is *Pippermint Get* which comes in a balloon-shaped bottle.

The Italian product *Mentuccia* is an herb blend characterized by caraway and mint flavors. See chapter on Caraway/Kümmel.

Schnapps is the German and Dutch name for any strong, dry spirit. *Peppermint Schnapps* is a dry, peppermint liquor. It is not a liqueur. *Tava* is an interesting American blend of mint, anise and orange flavors—lighter and drier than most liqueurs.

Mint/Peppermint

ASPARAGUS SUCCOTASH
Mint-flavored liqueurs add taste to
fresh-from-the-garden vegetables

2 cups corn fresh from the cob
2 cups cut asparagus spears, raw or cooked
1 cup milk
2 tablespoons butter or margarine
2 tablespoons all-purpose flour
1/2 teaspoon salt
4 teaspoons Tava or any mint-flavored liqueur
grated sharp cheese or Parmesan (optional)
dried bread crumbs (optional)

Cook corn and asparagus spears (if uncooked) in milk until *barely* tender. (This is a good way to use asparagus stalks while saving the tender tips for another use.) Melt butter and stir in flour, salt and Tava; add corn and asparagus with milk. Stir together well. Cook 5 minutes over medium heat before serving or sprinkle with grated cheese mixed with bread crumbs and bake for 30 minutes in a 350° oven.
Serves 6

MARGARET SCHRAMM'S MINTED LAMB
Fresh mint stuffing in a rolled leg of lamb
or piled upon chops

1/4 cup chopped onion
1/4 cup chopped celery
1/2 cup butter
2/3 cup fresh mint leaves, finely cut
4 cups dried bread crumbs
salt and pepper to taste
1 egg
1 7- to 8-pound leg of lamb, boned, or
    8 shoulder lamb chops
Crème de Menthe

Sauté onion and celery in butter. Stir together with mint leaves and bread crumbs. Season to taste and add egg. Brush the inside of the boned leg of lamb with Crème de Menthe and stuff; tie and roast 40 minutes per pound in a 350° oven. Or pile stuffing upon lamb chops which have been brushed with Crème de Menthe and bake 1 hour in a 350° oven.
Serves 8

MINT BUTTER
Lovely with lamb, peas, spinach

1/2 pound salted butter, softened
2 teaspoons clear or green Crème de Menthe
1 teaspoon dried mint leaves, crushed

Cut butter into mixing bowl; beat in Crème de Menthe and dried mint. Pack into individual pots or shape into 2 logs and roll in chopped fresh mint. Store in refrigerator or freezer.
Makes 1/2 pound

STRAWBERRY-STUFFED HONEYDEW
Melon filled with strawberries, iced and sliced

1 large honeydew melon
1 pint fresh strawberries
1/2 package (1-1/2 teaspoons) unflavored gelatin
1/4 cup cold water
1/2 cup Sauternes or Rhine wine
2 teaspoons orange-flavored liqueur
2 teaspoons frozen orange juice concentrate
1 8-ounce package cream cheese
2 teaspoons green Crème de Menthe
fresh mint

Peel melon down to edible meat. Cut a 3- or 4-inch diameter hole in one end so that you can reach inside and remove seeds with a spoon. Reserve cut-out portion. Wash and hull strawberries, reserving largest berries with hulls intact for decorating the whole melon when it has been frosted.

In a small saucepan combine gelatin with cold water, stirring to soften. Add wine and orange-flavored liqueur and heat, stirring to completely dissolve gelatin. Remove from heat and stir in juice concentrate together with 2 or 3 ice cubes. Cool until syrupy but not entirely set.

Place melon on end in a small bowl and arrange whole, hulled strawberries inside the melon, pouring in thickened gelatin as you work. Place in refrigerator until gelatin is set.

Place chilled melon on serving dish. You may need to slice the melon on one side or on the uncut end, depending upon whether you want it resting on its side or the end when it makes its grand appearance. Whip cream cheese with Crème de Menthe; use this icing to seal the cap to the melon and to frost the entire melon. Cut the reserved strawberries in half through their green hulls and arrange to suit your fancy as garnish on the frosted melon. Surround with fresh mint and chill before serving.
Serves 6 to 8

Mint/Peppermint

CRÈME DE MENTHE DIVINITY
Semisweet chocolate can be added for
a chocolate-mint surprise

2-1/2 cups granulated sugar
1/2 cup light corn syrup
1/2 cup cold water
2 egg whites
2-1/2 teaspoons green Crème de Menthe
1/4 cup chopped semisweet chocolate (optional)
1/2 cup chopped nuts

In a large saucepan combine sugar, corn syrup and water. Cook to soft ball stage (about 237°), stirring only until sugar dissolves. Meanwhile beat egg whites until stiff. When syrup reaches soft ball stage, gradually add half the syrup to egg whites while beating at high speed. Set aside. Cook remaining syrup to hard ball stage (about 260°) and slowly add to the egg whites, beating constantly. Add Crème de Menthe and, if you want the candy to be a light chocolate color, add the chocolate now. Beat until candy will hold its shape when dropped, about 5 minutes. Fold in nuts. Drop by teaspoons onto waxed paper or a lightly buttered surface.
Makes about 40 pieces

PULLED MINTS
The fun of a taffy pull with refreshing results

3 cups granulated sugar
1 cup water
2 tablespoons light corn syrup
1/4 teaspoon salt
1 tablespoon green or clear Crème de Menthe
1 cup sifted confectioners' sugar
1/2 cup cornstarch

Butter sides of a saucepan. Combine granulated sugar, water, corn syrup, salt and Crème de Menthe in the pan. Place over high heat and stir until sugar is dissolved and mixture reaches a boil. Continue cooking without stirring to the hard ball stage (about 260°). Remove from heat and pour onto a non-absorbent buttered surface. Cool until comfortable to handle (mixture should still be quite warm). Butter fingers and pull candy until it is light colored and glossy. Stretch into long ropes about 1/2-inch in diameter. With scissors cut into 1-inch pieces and drop at once into combined confectioners' sugar and cornstarch. Let stand in the mixture at room temperature overnight to mellow. Shake in a strainer to remove excess sugar mixture. When stored in an airtight container the candies will keep almost indefinitely.
Makes about 40 mints

DOUBLE CHOCOLATE MINT PUDDING
Thick Bittersweet Mocha Sauce and Crème de Menthe Whipped Cream cap the dark beauty

4 tablespoons butter or margarine
2/3 cup granulated sugar
1 egg
2-1/2 squares unsweetened chocolate, melted
2 cups all-purpose flour, spooned lightly into cup and leveled
1 tablespoon baking powder
1/2 teaspoon salt
3/4 cup milk
1/4 cup clear or green Crème de Menthe
Bittersweet Mocha Sauce, page 63
Crème de Menthe Whipped Cream, following

Cream butter and sugar together; beat in egg until well combined. Add melted chocolate. Mix together flour, baking powder and salt; sift into chocolate mixture alternately with milk and Crème de Menthe, beating after each addition. Scrape mixture into well-greased and floured 1-quart mold, filling no more than 3/4 full. Cover tightly. Steam 2 hours. Uncover and cool 10 minutes before unmolding. To reheat pudding, slip it into a buttered mold, cover and steam 1 hour. Serve with Bittersweet Mocha Sauce and Crème de Menthe Whipped Cream.
Serves 8 to 10

CRÈME DE MENTHE WHIPPED CREAM
Use the green liqueur for a pale green color

1 cup heavy cream
1/4 cup or less granulated sugar
1 tablespoon green Crème de Menthe

Whip cream until it begins to thicken; gradually beat in sugar. Add Crème de Menthe to taste.
Makes 2 cups

Baste lamb with a combination of Gin and Crème de Menthe.

Green Crème de Menthe makes a refreshing dessert served over chocolate or vanilla ice cream; sprinkle with candied mint leaves and garnish with a sprig of fresh mint.

𝔑uts

They're "the Nuts" in Cooking

ALL OF THE nut-flavored crèmes (most of the nut flavors are sold as crèmes) and liqueurs are very sweet and best used in desserts or with fruits. They're especially useful for flavoring icings, cake fillings, sweet breads and in dressings for fruit salads.

Noyau, Noyaux and *Crème de Noyau* are strong, sweet liqueurs whose almond flavor is extracted from peach and apricot kernels. This trio is available either bright red or clear white. They can tint, sweeten and flavor all in one fell swoop. The red is especially fun around Christmas and Valentine's Day.

Amaretto is an Italian almond-flavored liqueur that cooks extremely well. *Kola Liqueur,* made in Hawaii from kola nuts, citrus peels, tonka beans and vanilla, is another esoteric liqueur. *Nocino, Brou* and *Eau-de-Noix* are walnut liqueurs made by macerating the husks in Brandy with herbs and sugar syrup.

Coconut Whisqueur is a Scotch Whisky-based coconut liqueur produced mostly for use in the manufacture of European liqueur chocolates. Anyone who has visited the Caribbean is aware that the natives there brew a number of imaginative coconut-flavored liqueurs. *Coquito* is a beige coconut crème and *Campo Rico* is the coconut cream base for the area's popular Piña Colada cocktail.

Coconut and chocolate are a natural combination; both raised in the same warm-weather areas, they are often combined in a single liqueur. *Afri Koko* comes from the Congo and is very sweet and heavy. *Chococo* is a similar product from the Virgin Islands and *Coquito-Coco Ponche* is the Puerto Rican version of the combination.

A new liqueur, *Pistachia,* is flavored with pistachio nuts.

115

Nuts

SOUR CREAM NUT PIE
Almonds, walnuts, cashews or
macadamia nuts can be used

1 unbaked 9-inch pie shell, see Basics
1/4 pound butter or margarine
1/2 cup packed brown sugar
3/4 cup granulated sugar
4 eggs, beaten
1/2 teaspoon salt
1/2 cup sour cream
1/4 cup light corn syrup
1-1/2 teaspoons almond-flavored liqueur
1-1/2 cups nutmeats, coarsely chopped

Prepare 1 recipe Basic Pastry; use 1/4 of dough (about 1 cup) and shape dough into shell as directed in pastry recipe. Refrigerate or freeze remainder. Combine butter, sugars, eggs, salt, sour cream and corn syrup in a saucepan. Mix well and cook, stirring constantly, for about 5 minutes or until well blended. Remove from heat and add liqueur and nuts. Pour into pastry shell and bake in a preheated 350° oven for about 1 hour, until center is set.
Serves 8

NUTTY PEACHES
Plain Brandy will do, but the almond flavor of
Noyau is beautiful in this dish

6 to 8 fresh peaches*, or 1 #3 can homestyle
   peaches
blanched almonds
1 tablespoon Crème de Noyau
1 tablespoon Brandy

Arrange peach halves cut side up in a shallow baking dish, reserving liquid. Place several almonds in the center of each peach half. Add the Crème de Noyau and Brandy to the liquid from the peaches and pour over all. Bake in a 325° oven for about 2 hours. Baste every 30 minutes if you think of it (they will be good even if you forget). Serve warm with whipped cream to which you have added more of the Crème de Noyau.
Serves 6 to 8

*If using fresh peaches, peel, halve and pit them. Boil 1 cup water, 1/4 to 1/2 cup sugar and a dash of salt for 3 minutes. Lower heat, add peach halves and poach until tender.

SMOOTH FONDANT FOR STUFFING DRIED FRUITS
Can also be mixed with nuts and used
as the center for dipped chocolates

1/3 cup sweetened condensed milk
1 tablespoon Crème de Noyau, Kirsch or
    the liqueur of your choice
1/4 teaspoon vanilla extract
dash of salt
food coloring (optional)
2-1/2 to 3 cups sifted confectioners' sugar

Combine milk, flavorings, salt and food coloring.
Gradually blend in as much sugar as you can and
turn the candy out onto a surface heavily covered
with confectioners' sugar. Knead fondant, working
in sugar, until it is smooth and quite firm. Wrap in
foil and refrigerate to ripen at least 24 hours.
Makes enough to stuff 5 dozen dates or
3 dozen prunes which have been
marinated in Kirsch or orange-flavored liqueur

Liquor

RUM
COGNAC
WHISKY
BOURBON
GIN
VODKA
TEQUILA
BRANDY

Whiskey and Whisky

FOR THOSE who like the taste of *Whiskey,* or *Whisky,* but enjoy a bit of sweetness, too, the distillers add honey or sugar and often herbs, turning their products into liqueurs. Sweetened or unsweetened, flavored or "straight," Whiskies and Whisky liqueurs have been popular in the kitchen since Grandma started sneaking thimblefuls from Granddad's bottle to liven up her cooking. She no doubt found them delicious in mince pie, in the hard sauce served on the pie, in a steamed pudding or in her fruitcake batter. And she may have learned from her own Grandmother that a wee drop of straight Scotch, Irish Whiskey or Bourbon would enhance a hearty stew, a thick soup or a chewy, dark bread.

Whisky, or Whiskey, is distilled from fermented grain. Some varieties are flavored by the wood of the barrels they're aged in, some from whatever was stored in the barrels previously (old Sherry barrels are used for Scotch) and some from charring the barrels (Bourbon). There are a number of Whisky types, including Bourbon, corn, rye, straight, blended, Irish, Japanese, Canadian, Scotch and Malt. (The Scotch, true to their reputation for frugality, eliminate the extraneous "e" and so do the Canadians. So it's Scotch and Canadian Whisky but Irish or American Whiskey.) All may be used in cooking, chiefly with other strong flavors.

119

Whiskey and Whisky

WHISKY LIQUEURS

Drambuie is perhaps the most famous Whisky liqueur. It is reputed to be based upon a private recipe which Bonnie Prince Charlie gave to one of his Highland friends, Mackinnon of Strathaird for sheltering the hunted Prince when he lost the battle of Culloden Moor in 1745. The name Drambuie is Gaelic for "the drink that satisfies."

Another Scotch Whisky liqueur is *Glen Mist*—a blend of herbs, spices and honey with Scotch Whisky. Yet another is the well-known *Lochan Ora*, based upon Chivas Regal. *Glayva, Dewmiel* and *Clanrana* are other herb-and-spice liqueurs produced in Scotland.

Many of the Scotch Whisky makers produce liqueurs which are marketed under their brand names: *Pinch Liqueur, Cutty Sark Liqueur, Grant's Liqueur,* etc. These are generally very slightly sweetened and have no added flavoring. In addition there are Scotch-based liqueurs called *Spirit of Scotland, Scotch 'n' Orange* and probably many more. The distillers have capitalized upon the world-wide popularity of the smoky Scotch flavor and bring it to us in a variety of forms.

Irish Mist is a fairly dry liqueur based upon Irish Whiskey with heather honey as the sweetener. The recipe is said to be over 1,000 years old. It was the "Heather Wine" of the ancient Irish warriors. *Irish Coffee Liqueur* is mentioned in the coffee section.

Lindisfarne Liqueur is an English product made with honey and Whiskey, while *George M. Tiddy's Canadian Liqueur* is a light Canadian Whisky sweetened with sugar.

An American liqueur, *Rock and Rye,* is made from Rye Whiskey flavored by fruits which have been steeped in the spirit. It comes in two types: "Old-Fashioned" and "Milder." At one time it was sweetened with rock sugar candy crystallized onto a string—hence the name "Rock and Rye."

ERIN SOUP
Pass Whiskey or beer to flavor each bowlful

1/2 head green cabbage, cored and chopped
    (about 1/2 pound)
1 tablespoon butter or margarine
1 small onion, chopped
1 small potato, chopped
1/4 teaspoon mace
1 tablespoon flour
1-1/2 cups milk
1-1/2 cups chicken stock
1/2 teaspoon salt
freshly ground pepper
2 tablespoons Irish Whiskey
1 tablespoon chopped parsley
Irish Whiskey and beer for passing

Bring a kettle of water to boiling and stir in the cabbage. Turn off heat and let stand 5 minutes. Drain. Meanwhile melt butter in a heavy pan and sauté the chopped onion, without browning. Add potato and cabbage; stir in mace and flour. Gradually add the milk and chicken stock, bring to a boil and simmer 20 minutes until vegetables are tender. Purée in a blender or rub through a sieve. Reheat and add salt, pepper and Irish Whiskey to taste. If soup is too thick add more milk. Serve with chopped parsley sprinkled on top then pass the Irish Whiskey and/or beer to be stirred in to taste.
Serves 5 or 6

WINTER SQUASH SOUP WITH BOURBON
Serve it hot or cold

2 leeks or 1 small onion, diced
2 tablespoons butter or margarine
2 cups diced raw potatoes
2-1/2 cups half-and-half or milk
1-1/3 cups cooked, mashed winter squash
    (approximately 3/4 pound uncooked)
1 teaspoon salt
1/4 to 1/2 teaspoon ground pepper
3 tablespoons Seagram's 7 Crown or other Bourbon
French bread (optional)
Gruyère cheese (optional)
chopped peanuts (optional)

Sauté leeks or onions in butter until transparent but not browned. Add diced potatoes and milk; cook 20 minutes or until potatoes are tender. Purée in blender. Combine the purée with squash in a double boiler and season to taste with salt, pepper and Bourbon. Keep warm until serving time or chill and serve cold. If serving soup warm, spoon into warmed cups, top with a slice of French bread and a slice of Gruyère. Place under broiler to melt cheese and toast bread. Serve immediately.
Serves 6 to 8

Whiskey and Whisky

TIPSY SWEET POTATOES
Bourbon tips them into the unusual

2 medium sweet potatoes, baked or boiled, and
  peeled
3 tablespoons butter or margarine
2 tablespoons Bourbon Whiskey
1 tablespoon brown sugar
2 tablespoons chopped pecans

Whip cooked sweet potatoes with 2 tablespoons
butter, Bourbon and brown sugar. Stir in nuts and
place in buttered baking dish. Dot with remaining
butter and bake 20 to 30 minutes. Serve hot.
Serves 4

RUTABAGAS—IRISH STYLE
Make this in jig time with Irish Mist

1 medium-sized rutabaga
1/8 pound salt pork or slab bacon, finely diced
1 small onion, chopped
1 teaspoon Irish Mist
pepper
butter

Peel rutabaga and cut into small pieces. Cook in
boiling, very lightly salted water until tender.
Meanwhile, fry salt pork or bacon until brown and
crisp. Shortly before it is done, add onion and
cook a few minutes longer. Drain fat from the pork
and water from the rutabaga. Beat pork and rutabaga together with Irish Mist, pepper and butter
until light and fluffy.
Serves 4

EASTER VOL-AU-VENT FILLING
The giant French egg filled with ham, turkey, apples and nuts

1 Vol-Au-Vent pastry shell, see Basics
4 tablespoons butter or margarine
1/4 cup unsifted all-purpose flour
1/4 cup Bourbon
1-3/4 cups milk
1 teaspoon seasoning salt, see Basics
3/4 teaspoon dry mustard
few drops Worcestershire sauce
1 pound cooked ham, cut in cubes (about 1 cup)
1 cup cubed cooked turkey or chicken
1 cup raw apple chunks
1/2 to 1 cup whole walnuts

Prepare vol-au-vent shell as directed, using either Half-Puff or Puff Pastry recipe.

To make filling melt butter in a large saucepan; remove from heat and stir in flour. Gradually add Bourbon and milk, stirring to keep sauce free from lumps. Add seasonings and bring slowly to a boil, stirring constantly. Add remaining ingredients, except apples and nuts; keep mixture hot until ready to fill the vol-au-vent. Just before filling, stir in apple chunks and walnuts. Spoon into vol-au-vent, replace cap and serve as directed.
Serves 4 to 5

TOMATOES STUFFED WITH SMOKED SALMON
For brunch, for lunch, or as an appetizer

2 tomatoes
salt
freshly ground pepper
seasoning salt, see Basics
2 tablespoons finely chopped onion
1 tablespoon butter
2 ounces smoked salmon
1/2 teaspoon Irish Whiskey
2 tablespoons sour cream
parsley or watercress

Wash tomatoes, slice off tops and scoop out centers, leaving about 1/2-inch shells. Cut a hole in each tomato top, removing tough section where tomato was attached to vine. Sprinkle tomato shells liberally with salt, pepper and seasoning salt.

Sauté onion in butter; stir in smoked salmon and Irish Whiskey. Spoon into tomato shells, cover with tomato tops and broil a few moments. Remove from broiler, lift tops and spoon in sour cream. Replace tops and place a sprig of parsley or watercress in each hole. Serve hot.
Serves 2

Whiskey and Whisky

SQUAB-STUFFED SQUAB
One squab stuffs two others

3 squab

Marinade:
1 cup dry red wine
1 carrot, thinly sliced
parsley sprigs
1 small onion, thinly sliced
1 tablespoon Gin

Stuffing:
1 small onion, chopped
1/2 cup coarsely chopped fresh mushrooms
   (stems will do)
3 tablespoons butter or margarine
julienne strips of uncooked meat from
   the third squab
1/4 cup pignolias or broken pecans
3/4 cup cooked brown or white rice
1 egg
1 tablespoon Scotch Whisky
3/4 teaspoon salt
1/4 teaspoon coriander
freshly ground pepper

Flambé:
1/4 cup Brandy or Cognac

To bone: The birds don't absolutely have to be boned, but boning is a simple task which makes eating much easier. To do the job, cut through the skin along the backbone, then run a small, sharp knife between meat and bone, leaving meat attached to the skin and taking care not to tear the meat. As you come to the wings and legs, disjoint them but leave the bones in them. Continue to cut, freeing the body cavity of bone. When completely loosened remove rib cage intact.

To marinate: Combine marinade ingredients. Wash birds and place in a bowl with the marinade for 1 hour or overnight; turn occasionally. (Marinating can be done either before or after boning.)

To stuff: Sauté onion and mushrooms for the stuffing in butter; combine with strips of squab and the remaining ingredients. Spread the 2 boned birds open, skin side down. Divide the stuffing between the birds. Pull the backs together and slightly overlap the skin. Skewer if desired, though it is not necessary.

To bake: Turn each bird breast side up on doubled aluminum foil slightly larger than the bird. Fold wing tips back under the top part of the bodies and tie the legs together. Fold foil from sides and ends up under the birds to make small, almost invisible nests which hold the birds in place during cooking. Total roasting time is 45 minutes. Place uncovered birds with "nests" in a roasting pan and slip into a preheated 350° oven for 10 minutes. Then baste the birds with the marinade, cover the pan and roast for 20 minutes. Baste again and complete the last 15 minutes of cooking period uncovered.

To serve: Warm Brandy or Cognac, ignite and pour over the birds.

Serves 2 or 3

Whiskey and Whisky

CORK STEAK
A rich Irish Whiskey sauce
flavors thin slices of steak

1/3 pound tenderloin, or other tender beef, cut
 into 1/4-inch slices
1 tablespoon butter
1/4 cup sliced fresh mushrooms
1/4 cup heavy cream
1 teaspoon Irish Whiskey
salt
Worcestershire sauce

Pan-fry steak slices in butter to desired doneness;
remove meat from pan and keep warm; sauté
mushrooms in remaining butter. Stir in heavy
cream, scraping pan bottom; heat through but do
not boil. Add Irish Whiskey, salt to taste and a
drop or two of Worcestershire sauce. Pour sauce
over steak slices and serve.
Serves 1; multiply proportions
by number of people being served

IRISH FARMHOUSE STEW
Lamb stew thickened with potatoes
and flavored with Irish Whiskey

Broth:
bones and trimmings from 2-1/2 pounds lamb
 stew meat
2 cups cold water
1 small onion
1 celery top

Stew:
2 pounds lamb stew meat, cut in chunks
1 small garlic clove, crushed
1/2 teaspoon light brown or raw sugar
pinch thyme
freshly ground black pepper
1 cup finely shredded or blender-chopped
 raw potato
1/4 cup Irish Whiskey
3 medium potatoes
6 carrots
6 small whole onions, peeled
1-1/2 teaspoons salt
beef broth

Broth: Place all lamb trimmings except skin in heavy saucepan with water, onion and celery top. Simmer about 1/2 hour. Strain; skim off fat and reserve liquid for stew.

Stew: Brown lamb meat with some oil. Place in stew pot with next 6 ingredients and reserved broth to cover. Cover and cook slowly about 1-1/2 hours. Liquid will be slightly thickened and shredded potatoes will have entirely disappeared. Cut and trim potatoes and carrots to the size of the onions; add all three vegetables and salt. Cook, covered, 30 minutes longer or until vegetables are tender. Add any remaining lamb broth or some beef broth if mixture becomes too thick.

Serves 6

IRISH WHISKEY BROWN BREAD
It's a mellow loaf

2 cups whole-wheat flour
1-1/3 cups unsifted all-purpose flour
1 teaspoon salt
1 teaspoon baking soda
1 teaspoon sugar
2 tablespoons butter or bacon fat
1 cup buttermilk or sour milk
1/2 cup Irish Whiskey

Preheat oven to 425°. In a bowl stir together the flours, salt, baking soda and sugar. With a pastry blender cut in the butter. Combine liquids and stir in until just blended. Turn dough onto floured surface and knead lightly to shape into a ball. Place on lightly oiled baking sheet and cut a deep cross on the top of the loaf so that the slashes run down the sides of the ball. Bake 40 minutes or until loaf sounds hollow when tapped on the bottom.

Makes 1 loaf

Whiskey and Whisky

SOUR MASH SQUASH BREAD
A nutty bread which does double duty as a dessert

4 eggs
3 cups granulated sugar
1 cup salad oil
1-1/2 teaspoons salt
1 teaspoon ground cinnamon
1 teaspoon ground nutmeg
1-1/3 cups cooked winter squash
   (approximately 3/4 pound uncooked)
1/4 cup Sour Mash Whiskey
1 tablespoon orange-flavored liqueur
2 teaspoons baking soda
3 cups unsifted all-purpose flour,
   spooned into cup and leveled
1 cup chopped pecans

Preheat oven to 350°. Butter and flour 3 tall 1-pound coffee cans or 3 loaf pans. Beat together eggs, sugar, oil, salt, cinnamon and nutmeg. Add squash, Whiskey and liqueur. When mixture is smooth, add baking soda and then the flour, 1 cup at a time, beating only to combine. Stir in pecans and pour into prepared containers. Bake 1 hour or until toothpick inserted in center comes out clean. Slide bread out of cans or pans while still warm. Cool. To store, slip back into pans or cans and cover with can lid or with foil.
Makes 3 loaves

TENNESSEE WHISKEY BREAD
A sour-mash match for any meal

1/2 cup raisins
water to cover
3-1/2 tablespoons Tennessee Sour Mash Whiskey
2 cups unsifted all-purpose flour, spooned
   lightly into cup and leveled
1 tablespoon baking powder
1/2 teaspoon salt
3 tablespoons sugar
3 tablespoons butter
2 eggs
1/2 cup milk

Preheat oven to 350° and generously butter a bread pan. In a saucepan cover raisins with water, add 2 tablespoons Sour Mash Whiskey and simmer 5 minutes; drain and cool. Sift together into a bowl the flour, baking powder, salt and sugar. With a pastry blender cut in butter to the fineness of coarse meal. Beat eggs and milk together; add raisins and 1-1/2 tablespoons Whiskey. Pour egg-raisin mixture into dry ingredients and stir until just combined. Turn into pan (the batter will be very thick); bake 45 to 50 minutes, until a toothpick inserted in center comes out clean. Do not overbake. Cool 5 minutes. Remove from pan to cooling rack.
Makes 1 loaf

BOURBON PUFF
A cooked frosting flavored with Bourbon

3 egg whites
1-1/2 cups packed light brown sugar
1/4 teaspoon salt
1/4 cup cold water
2 tablespoons Bourbon
1/2 cup chopped pecans or walnuts (optional)

Combine all ingredients except nuts in the top of a double boiler and place over boiling water. Beat continuously with an electric mixer until frosting thickens and holds peaks well. Fold in more than half of the nuts. Use frosting to fill and frost cake. Sprinkle remaining nuts on entire top of cake or on rim only.

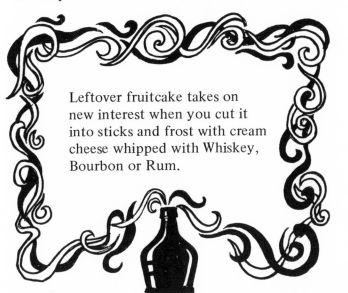

Leftover fruitcake takes on new interest when you cut it into sticks and frost with cream cheese whipped with Whiskey, Bourbon or Rum.

CHESTNUT SOUFFLÉ
Light and fluffy with a nutty texture

1/2 pound raw chestnuts, shelled and ground
3/4 cup granulated sugar
1/8 teaspoon ground cinnamon
1/8 teaspoon salt
1 teaspoon Lochan Ora or Drambuie
3 eggs, separated
Rum Caramel Sauce, page 150

To prepare chestnuts, cut a 1-inch slit on the flat side, cover with cold water and bring to a boil. Boil 1 minute only. Leave the chestnuts in the water as you proceed to peel them. A blender works well for grinding the shelled nuts.

Preheat oven to 325°. Butter and collar a 1-quart soufflé dish (butter the inside of the collar well also). Cream together the sugar, cinnamon, salt, liqueur and egg yolks; stir in ground chestnuts. Whip egg whites until very stiff. Using a wire whip, fold together with the chestnut mixture. Pour into prepared soufflé dish and bake 35 minutes at 325°. Raise oven temperature to 375° for 5 minutes and then to 400° for the final 5 minutes. Serve immediately with warm Rum Caramel Sauce and thick cream.
Serves 4

Whiskey and Whisky

IRISH COTTAGE CAKE
Apple slices sandwiched between tender scone crusts

Scones:
3 cups sifted all-purpose flour
1/2 cup granulated sugar
1 teaspoon salt
1 teaspoon baking soda
1 teaspoon ground nutmeg
grated rind of 1/2 lemon
4 tablespoons butter
1 cup buttermilk or sour milk

Filling:
3 large or 4 small cooking apples
1-1/2 tablespoons Irish Whiskey
1/4 cup firmly packed raw sugar or light
   brown sugar
2 tablespoons butter

Topping:
milk or half-and-half
1 tablespoon granulated sugar
1/4 teaspoon ground cinnamon

Irish Mist Sauce, following
heavy cream

Scones: Preheat oven to 400°. Sift together into a bowl the flour, sugar, salt, baking soda and nutmeg. Stir in lemon rind. Blend in butter with a pastry blender or 2 knives. Add enough buttermilk to make a soft dough. Turn onto a floured surface
130

and knead lightly 8 to 10 times, until dough holds together well. Divide in 2 parts and roll out one half to fit a 9-inch square pan, with a little of the dough coming part way up the sides.
Filling: Peel, core and thinly slice the apples. Arrange the slices on top of the scone dough in the pan; sprinkle with Whiskey and sugar; dot with butter. Roll remaining dough to cover the apple slices. Pat into place and press edges together to seal. With a skewer prick the top of the cake to the apples, but not through to the bottom.
Topping: Brush the top with milk and sprinkle with combined sugar and cinnamon. Bake 50 to 60 minutes. Serve with Irish Mist Sauce and heavy cream.
Serves 6 to 9

IRISH MIST SAUCE
As ethereal as mist rising from the moor

1 cup granulated sugar
2 tablespoons plus 2 teaspoons cornstarch
1/4 teaspoon salt
1/4 teaspoon ground cinnamon
3 cups water
1 tablespoon Irish Mist

Combine the dry ingredients in a saucepan. Gradually stir in water and Irish Mist. Place over medium heat and stir constantly until sauce comes to a boil; simmer 5 minutes. Serve warm on any apple dessert.
Makes 3 cups

ROCK AND RYE SQUASH PIE
Much like pumpkin but more subtly flavored

pastry for a single-crust pie, see Basics
3 eggs
1-1/3 cups cooked and mashed winter squash
2/3 cup granulated sugar
1/2 teaspoon salt
3/4 teaspoon ground cinnamon
3/4 teaspoon ground ginger
1/2 teaspoon ground nutmeg
1/2 teaspoon ground allspice
1/4 teaspoon ground cloves
1-1/4 cups evaporated milk
1/4 cup Rock and Rye

Preheat oven to 425°. Prepare 1 recipe Basic Pastry and use 1/4 of dough for shell; refrigerate or freeze remainder. Roll out dough as directed in recipe and line a 9-inch pie pan. Pierce shell with tines of fork and bake for 10 to 12 minutes. Cool.

To make the filling, beat the eggs lightly and combine with squash, sugar, salt, spices, evaporated milk and Rock and Rye. Pour into pastry shell. Bake 15 minutes at 425° and then reduce heat to 350°. Bake 40 to 50 minutes longer or until knife inserted in center comes out clean.
Serves 6 to 8

Whiskey and Whisky

MANHATTAN HOLIDAY PUDDING
Flavored the Manhattan cocktail way

1/2 cup currants
1/2 cup sweet Vermouth or Cream Sherry
3 cups torn stale bread (3 to 4 slices),
    cake or cookie crumbs
1-1/2 cups heavy cream
1 cup granulated sugar
1-1/2 cups unsifted all-purpose flour
1 teaspoon salt
1-1/2 teaspoons baking powder
1/2 teaspoon baking soda
1/2 cup glacéed pineapple
1/2 cup snipped dates
1/2 cup snipped dried figs
1/2 cup snipped dried apricots
1/2 cup halved glacéed cherries
1 cup slivered or sliced almonds
1 cup chopped pecans
1/4 cup Bourbon Whiskey
Fluffy Bourbon Hard Sauce, following

Soak currants in Vermouth or Sherry overnight or longer. Combine torn bread or crumbs with heavy cream in a large bowl to soften while combining dry ingredients, fruit and nuts in another bowl. Heat Bourbon in a small pan and ignite to burn off alcohol and reduce volume. Add currants and wine to bread and cream, beating well with electric mixer to break up crumbs. Add reduced Bourbon, then stir in dry ingredients. Mix thoroughly and pour into well greased and floured 2-quart mold. Cover tightly and steam 3 hours. Uncover, cool and remove from mold. When pudding has completely cooled, wrap it in cheesecloth (or any cotton fabric) which has been well soaked in Vermouth or Sherry. Then wrap twice in foil to keep as airtight as possible. Refrigerate about 1 month. Reheat to serve and top with Fluffy Bourbon Hard Sauce.
Serves 12 to 14

FLUFFY BOURBON HARD SAUCE
A very saucy sauce

1 cup granulated sugar
1 tablespoon butter or margarine
2 tablespoons heavy cream
1 tablespoon Bourbon, or to taste
3 egg whites, stiffly beaten

Cream together sugar and butter, beat in cream and Bourbon. Fold together with egg whites. The sauce will separate so combine egg whites with Bourbon mixture just before serving.
Makes about 2 cups

VINARTERTA
A multilayered Icelandic cookie-cake

1/2 pound butter or margarine
1 cup granulated sugar
2 eggs
4 cups unsifted all-purpose flour, spooned
    lightly into cup and leveled
2 teaspoons baking powder
1/2 teaspoon salt
1/4 cup milk
1 tablespoon Bourbon
Prune Filling, following
additional Bourbon or spirit of choice
1/4 cup chopped walnuts

Preheat oven to 350°. In a large bowl, cream butter and sugar together until light and fluffy. Add eggs one at a time and blend well. Combine dry ingredients and add alternately with milk to butter mixture, stirring well after each addition. Add Bourbon. Bake "cookie-cakes" in batches of 2 or 3 at a time (depending on the size of your oven). To make each layer, spread about 1/8 of the dough thinly with a rubber scraper on the surface of a buttered upside-down pie tin or layer cake pan. Do not extend dough over edges of pan. Bake 20 minutes, remove from oven and cool for 5 minutes. Remove cookie from pan and cool completely on a rack. Then reuse pans, baking layers until dough is used up.

Assemble Vinarterta on a baking sheet or other flat surface. Spread each layer with Prune Filling and sprinkle lightly with a little Bourbon or spirit of your choice. Place one on top of the other and decorate the top with chopped nuts. Wrap the cake in foil and store at least 24 hours. Vinarterta keeps 2 weeks or longer. To serve cut into small portions; the Scandinavian way is to cut it into blocks, not wedges.
Makes a multilayered cake
which will serve 20 or more

PRUNE FILLING
*Can be made with any other dried fruit or
a combination of fruits such as apricot and prune*

1-1/2 pounds pitted prunes, chopped
1-1/2 cups granulated sugar
1 cup water
1/4 teaspoon salt
4 cardamom seeds
1/4 cup Bourbon or Rock and Rye
1 tablespoon dry Sherry

Combine fruit, sugar, water and salt in a saucepan and simmer, stirring occasionally, until fruit is tender and soft. Then the undrained mixture may be used as is, if the initial chopping was fine enough, or it can be puréed. Crush cardamom and remove the white husks; blend cardamom, Bourbon and Sherry into the cooled fruit before spreading on the Vinarterta layers.

Brandy and Cognac

Brandy is a spirit made by distilling either wine or a fermented mash of a fruit other than grapes and aging the distillate in wood. Grape Brandies are frequently identified by place of origin and other fruit Brandies by the name of the fruit. Examples are: *Cognac* (from one particular region of France named Cognac, hence Cognac is always capitalized where Brandy need not be), *Armagnac* (produced southeast of Bordeaux in Gers and aged in black oak), *Spanish Brandy, Israeli Brandy,* etc. Fruit Brandies and fruit-flavored Brandies are discussed in the chapter on Fruit.

Any of the Brandies and Cognacs are excellent in so many dishes that a bottle of inexpensive Brandy should be on hand in the kitchen at all times. Brandies from different countries tend to vary greatly in flavor—chiefly, perhaps, from the barrels they are aged in, but also from the grapes used in the original distillation. Spanish and Greek Brandies are very distinctive and very good in cooking, particularly meats.

Many flavored liqueurs are based upon grape Brandy or Cognac, but occasionally the flavor of the Brandy or Cognac itself is the basic flavor in a liqueur. *Honey Brandy* is an example. This ancient drink trickled down to us from the Anglo-Saxons who fermented honey to make *Mead,* which was about eight percent alcohol. The Welsh added spices to the Mead and called it *Metheglin. Hydromel* (honey water) was the Roman equivalent. Today when Mead has been distilled it is called Honey Brandy. Flavorings are sometimes added and, of course, different honeys have various flavors; you just taste your way along when cooking with them.

Brandy and Cognac

ORANGE DUCKLING TERRINE
*Pâté alternates with strips of marinated breast of
duck—a well-seasoned gelatin
binds all into a delightful appetizer*

1 duckling

Marinade:
2 tablespoons Cognac or Brandy
juice of 3 oranges
grated rind of 1/2 orange
2 shallots, finely chopped
1/4 teaspoon salt
1 teaspoon dried thyme
1 bay leaf, crushed

Pâté:
7/8 cup (7 ounces) ground duck or chicken liver
7/8 cup (7 ounces) ground lean veal
7/8 cup (7 ounces) ground lean pork
7/8 cup (7 ounces) ground lean bacon
1 teaspoon unflavored gelatin powder
1 egg
1/4 cup chopped parsley
1 1-ounce can truffles, chopped
1 tablespoon salt
fresh ground pepper (white preferred)
orange slices

Gelatin:
bouillon
salt
pepper
orange juice
Madeira
unflavored gelatin powder
cold water

Marinade: Skin and bone the duck. Cut breast meat in thin strips. Combine all marinade ingredients. Marinate strips for 12 hours; drain.

Pâté: Grind liver, veal, pork, bacon and the portions of duck meat not in marinade together twice. (Do not discard carcass or other scraps of duck.) Add the marinade liquid, gelatin powder, egg, parsley, truffles with can juices, salt and pepper. Mix well, let stand 30 minutes and press mixture into a well-greased 8-cup terrine dish, alternating layers of pâté and breast strips and making certain to both begin and end with pâté. Cover terrine tightly with foil or a lid. Set in a pan of hot water (bain-marie) with water coming halfway up side of terrine. Bake at 350° for 1-1/2 hours. Remove terrine from bain-marie and pour off all fluids. Place a weight on the mixture (cans of food or a brick work well) and put terrine on a rack to cool. When terrine has cooled, decorate the top with very thin half-slices of orange.

Gelatin: While the terrine is cooking make a bouillon by simmering the duck carcass and leftover parts of the duck in water to cover seasoned with salt and pepper for 1-1/2 hours. Strain the bouillon, add orange juice and Madeira to taste. Measure the liquid and add gelatin which has been softened in a small amount of cold water, allowing 1 envelope of gelatin per pint of liquid (1 pint should be adequate for the terrine). Bring the mixture to a boil, cool and pour around and just barely over the meat. When the gelatin has set, the terrine may be unmolded for serving or left in the terrine dish for storage in a cool place. Serve on any kind of salad green, garnish with tiny sour pickles cut the long way to fan out. Or serve with a Cumberland Sauce (see Basics).

Serves 8 to 12

Brandy and Cognac

CHICKEN LIVER-MUSHROOM PÂTÉ
WITH COGNAC
Honor guests with a creamy "handmade" pâté

1 pound chicken livers
1/2 pound fresh mushrooms, sliced
1/3 cup finely chopped green onions
1 clove garlic, pressed
1 teaspoon paprika
4 tablespoons butter or margarine
1/3 cup dry white wine
1/4 teaspoon dill weed
3 drops Tabasco sauce
1/4 pound butter
1/4 cup Cognac
salt
clarified butter* (optional)
sieved egg white and minced parsley (optional)

Sauté chicken livers, mushrooms, green onions, garlic and paprika in the 4 tablespoons butter until onions are cooked through. Add white wine, dill weed and Tabasco; cover and cook slowly 10 minutes longer. Cool and whirl, one half at a time, in the blender, blending 4 tablespoons butter, 2 tablespoons Cognac and salt to taste into each batch. Put into pots to cool and cover tops with a thin layer of clarified butter. If pâté is being served the day it is made it does not need to be sealed with butter. Instead sprinkle sieved egg white over one half of each pot of pâté and minced parsley over the other half, holding a piece of paper in place vertically to keep them separated as you sprinkle. Serves 6 to 8

*To clarify butter, melt it over a very low heat. Pour the clear liquid which appears on top off; it is "clarified." Use the bottom butter with the whitish deposit for other cooking.

138

TURKEY-HAM PÂTÉ
Individual pots can be frozen for future use

1/3 cup chopped green pepper
4 shallots, chopped
1/3 cup chopped parsley
1/2 pound butter
1 tablespoon Durkees Famous Sauce
3 cups finely ground cooked turkey or
  chicken (3/4 pound)
1 cup finely ground cooked ham (1/4 pound)
1 cup heavy cream
3/4 cup dry white wine
2 tablespoons Cognac
truffle slices (optional)

Sauté green pepper, shallots and parsley in 1/4 pound butter. Add Durkees Sauce, turkey or chicken and ham. Combine liquids and place about 1/3 of liquids in blender with about 1/3 of meat mixture and blend until smooth; repeat with remaining ingredients. Melt the remaining 1/4 pound butter. Clarify by pouring off the clear portion and use the clear butter to seal the top of the pâté in small pots. If desired decorate with truffle slices before the butter solidifies.
Makes about 5 cups

Brandy and Cognac

COGNAC BUTTER
*Serve with broiled lobster, beef or lamb and
as a topping for peas, broccoli or cauliflower*

1/2 pound salted butter, softened
4 teaspoons Cognac or other Brandy
2 teaspoons dried chives or 3 teaspoons
   fresh chopped chives
1/4 teaspoon dried dill weed or 1/2 teaspoon
   chopped fresh dill
additional chopped chives and dill

Cut butter into mixing bowl; beat in Cognac,
chives and dill. Pack into individual butter pots or
shape into logs and roll in additional snipped dill
and chives. Chill or freeze.
Makes 1/2 pound

ROQUEFORT BUTTER
*Cognac or Brandy makes this
excellent on grilled meats*

1/2 pound salted butter, softened
1 tablespoon softened Roquefort or blue cheese
1 tablespoon Cognac or Brandy
1/2 teaspoon Worcestershire sauce
coarsely cracked black pepper (optional)

Cut butter and cheese into mixing bowl; beat in
liquids. Pack into individual pots or shape into 2
logs and roll in coarsely cracked black pepper.
Makes 1/2 pound

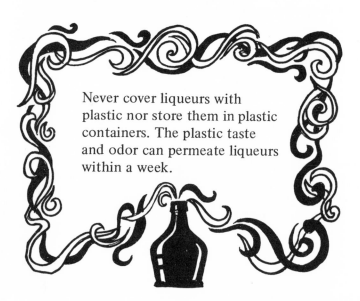

Never cover liqueurs with
plastic nor store them in plastic
containers. The plastic taste
and odor can permeate liqueurs
within a week.

UNUSUAL LOBSTER SOUFFLÉ
The cheese soufflé rests on lobster sauce with additional sauce spooned over at serving time

butter
2 tablespoons grated Parmesan cheese

Lobster Sauce:
2 tablespoons chopped shallots
1 tablespoon chopped parsley
2 tablespoons butter or margarine
1 cup chopped cooked lobster meat
1 tablespoon Cognac
1/4 cup dry white wine
1/2 cup heavy cream

Soufflé:
2 tablespoons butter or margarine
2 tablespoons flour
2 tablespoons milk
2 egg yolks, beaten
1/2 cup grated Swiss, Parmesan or mild
   Cheddar cheese
1/4 teaspoon salt
dash cayenne
3 or 4 egg whites
1/8 teaspoon cream of tartar

Preheat oven to 350°. Prepare a 3-cup soufflé dish with a 1-inch or higher collar. Butter the dish and the inside rim of the collar. Sprinkle with Parmesan cheese.
Lobster Sauce: Sauté shallots and parsley in butter; add lobster meat, Cognac, wine and cream. Simmer gently for 15 minutes.
Soufflé: In another saucepan melt butter, stir in flour to make a roux and slowly stir in milk, eliminating any lumps. Cook until simmering and thickened. Whip a little of the hot mixture into the egg yolks and then add egg yolk mixture to the saucepan. Add cheese, salt and cayenne, stirring constantly until the cheese is melted. Remove from heat. Beat egg whites together with cream of tartar until stiff but not dry. Fold egg yolk mixture into egg whites.

Spoon half of lobster sauce mixture into bottom of the prepared soufflé dish, cover with soufflé and bake 20 minutes at 350°. Increase temperature to 400° for 10 minutes longer or until soufflé is golden. Serve immediately with remaining lobster mixture as a sauce.
Serves 2 to 3

Brandy and Cognac

BIFTECK AU POIVRE
A less expensive version of the classic French dish

2 pounds lean ground beef
4 teaspoons coarsely cracked black pepper*
salt
4 tablespoons butter
1/8 teaspoon Tabasco sauce
1 teaspoon Worcestershire sauce
1 teaspoon lemon juice
2 tablespoons warm Cognac

Shape beef into patties and press each patty down onto cracked pepper. Sprinkle pan bottom with salt and cook burgers until well browned on both sides. Reduce heat and add remaining ingredients except Cognac to the pan. Cook meat to desired degrees of rareness and remove from pan. Set the Cognac aflame and pour into the skillet, scraping pan bottom to loosen browned particles. Pour sauce over the patties and serve.
Serves 4

*Coarsely cracked black pepper can be purchased, or you can adjust your pepper mill to a coarse grind, or you can place whole peppercorns in the folded corner of a towel and smash with a hammer.

PICNIC GAME HENS
A meaty stuffing flavored with Cognac

8 Rock Cornish game hens
salt and pepper
8 livers from the hens
1/4 pound butter
8 medium mushrooms, sliced
1-1/2 cups finely chopped cooked ham
2 cups torn bread
1/4 cup chopped pistachio nuts
2 tablespoons Cognac
1/4 cup dry white wine
2 tablespoons red currant, chokecherry or
   quince jelly

Preheat oven to 350°. Liberally salt and pepper the cavities of the game hens. Gently sauté the livers in 4 tablespoons of the butter; remove from pan and finely chop. Sauté the mushrooms in pan juices; combine with chopped livers, chopped ham, bread, pistachio nuts and Cognac. Stuff lightly into body cavity. Tie each bird's legs to close the cavity and roast 45 minutes. Meanwhile combine the remaining 4 tablespoons butter, white wine and jelly; heat together until melted and smooth. Baste hens occasionally with this sauce while roasting. After 45 minutes increase temperature to 425° and roast an additional 10 to 15 minutes until birds are nicely browned.
Serves 8

HARVEST KETTLE
A chicken-vegetable stew
spiked with Spanish Brandy

1 large chicken, cut into 8 small portions
3 cups strong beef broth
2 cups water
2 yams, peeled and cut into 1/2-inch thick rounds
1 cup peeled and diced pumpkin or
    Hubbard squash
2 ears corn, cut into 6 rounds each
6 small onions
1 to 3 small fresh chilies, rinsed, stemmed,
    seeded and chopped (or 3 to 5 canned
    hot chilies, chopped)*
1 teaspoon salt
freshly ground black pepper
1/3 cup flour
1/2 cup Spanish Brandy
1 cup peas or chopped broccoli (fresh or frozen)

Combine chicken, beef broth and water in a Dutch oven and bring to a boil; reduce heat and simmer 45 minutes. Add vegetables except peas or broccoli and seasonings, then cook 15 minutes longer. Combine flour with Brandy and a little additional water to make a smooth paste. Stir in some of the hot stock from the pot and then add mixture to the chicken, blending well. Add peas or broccoli. Stir occasionally for the next 5 minutes. Test vegetables for doneness and serve from the pot or in a heated tureen.
Serves 6

*These chilies are *very* hot. Begin with 1 and taste your way along.

Rum

Rum is another almost indispensible bottle for the kitchen collection. The product itself has many variations, running from the heavy, dark, full-flavored Rums which you might use in anything where molasses would be welcome—baked beans, baked ham, gingerbread—to the very light, very delicately flavored Rums which are currently being touted for the Rum martini and allied drinks. The lighter Rums are excellent in chiffon pies, icings on spice cakes or cookies, in chicken dishes, etc.—where just a hint of the Rum flavor would be welcome.

Rum is a distillate of products of fermented sugarcane. Of all the spirits it retains the most natural flavor of its origins, though the "light Rum" makers are busy trying to take the flavor away. The light and dry Rums are distilled originally at high proof and then diluted, while the dark and very flavorful Rums are distilled at low proof. The *very* high-proof Rums (151° proof, about 75 percent alcohol) are designed for flambéing. The sweetened Rum liqueurs are mentioned in the chapters dealing with their principal flavors.

Rum

RUM RUNNER YAMS
Dark Rum and orange flavor the vegetable

5 medium oranges
4 large yams, cooked, or 2 1-pound, 1-ounce
   cans yams
1/4 cup packed brown sugar
2 tablespoons dark Rum
1 teaspoon salt
1/4 teaspoon ground cinnamon
1/8 teaspoon ground nutmeg
1/8 teaspoon ground ginger
1 egg

Make a saw-tooth cut around oranges to divide them in half. Clean out the shells, using a grapefruit knife to cut out most of the edible portion. Remove seeds and cut pulp into small pieces.

Mash yams; add the remaining ingredients and orange bits (an electric mixer does the job quickly). Pile mashed yams into empty orange shells and refrigerate until 30 minutes before serving time. Bake in 350° oven until nicely browned and warmed through the center.
Serves 8 to 10

RUM BAKED BEANS
Brown and beautiful—full of flavor

1 pound dried Great Northern beans (2 to
   2-1/2 cups)
water
1 small onion, coarsely chopped
1/2 pound slab bacon or salt pork, cut in
   large dice
1/4 cup dark molasses
1/4 cup catsup
1 tablespoon dry mustard
2 teaspoons salt
2 tablespoons dark Rum

Cover beans with water and bring them slowly to the boiling point, or cover with water and soak 12 hours. Drain beans, cover again with water, and simmer long and slowly until the skin of a bean will burst when you blow on it.

Drain beans, saving water. Add remaining ingredients and mix together in a roaster or bean pot, adding bean water to barely cover. Bake, covered, in a 250° oven 6 to 8 hours. If beans become dry, add a little more water. Uncover for the last hour of cooking.
Makes 1-1/2 quarts, about 6 good-sized portions

RUM BUTTER
Delightful with ham, sweet potatoes, squash

1/2 pound salted butter, softened
2 tablespoons plus 2 teaspoons dark Rum
1/4 teaspoon ground nutmeg
whole cloves (optional)

Cut butter into mixing bowl; beat in Rum and nutmeg. Pack into individual pots or shape into 2 logs and stud with whole cloves just before serving. Store in refrigerator or freezer.

The lighter Rum is in color, the less strong the flavor.

Add dark Rum and molasses to baked beans.

ORANGE-RUM FONDUE
A honey of a dessert

4 tablespoons butter
1/2 cup heavy cream
2 tablespoons granulated sugar
2 tablespoons honey (orange blossom preferred)
2 tablespoons orange marmalade
2 tablespoons medium Rum
fruits of choice*

Combine butter, cream, sugar, honey and marmalade. Bring to a full, foaming boil, stirring vigorously; cook 30 seconds. Add the Rum and keep warm over very low heat. Dip fruits into the sauce and eat fondue style.

*This is especially good with peaches, pineapple, bananas, grapes, strawberries, papayas, mangoes.

Rum

RUM BUNS
They'll vanish without a crumb of evidence

Filling:
1 cup dark raisins
dark Rum
1-1/2 cups granulated sugar
2 tablespoons ground cinnamon
1/2 teaspoon ground nutmeg
4 tablespoons soft butter

Buns:
1 package dry yeast
1/2 cup lukewarm water
7/8 cup milk
2 tablespoons dark Rum
1/3 cup melted shortening
1/3 cup granulated sugar
2 teaspoons salt
1 egg
5 to 5-1/2 cups unsifted flour

confectioners' sugar
heavy cream
reserved Rum

Filling: Cover raisins with dark Rum and let stand until buns are shaped. In a small bowl combine sugar, cinnamon and nutmeg; set aside.

Buns: Combine yeast and 1/2 cup water in a large bowl to soften yeast granules. Heat milk and Rum together until bubbles begin to form around edge of saucepan. Remove from heat and add shortening, sugar and salt, stirring to melt the shortening and dissolve the sugar and salt. Cool. Add egg and 2 cups of the flour to dissolved yeast; combine thoroughly (you can use an electric mixer). Add the cooled milk-Rum mixture, blending it in well. Gradually work in more flour to make a soft dough. Turn onto floured surface. Knead 10 minutes, adding flour as required to prevent sticking. Oil both a large bowl and the surface of the ball of dough. Cover and store in refrigerator or shape immediately into Rum Buns.

When baking refrigerated dough allow about 2 hours for shaping, rising and baking; unrefrigerated dough requires about 1-1/2 hours. Drain raisins, saving Rum to use in icing. Roll out 1/4 of the dough at a time, shaping rectangles 1/4 inch thick. Spread each rectangle with 1 tablespoon of butter. Sprinkle about 1/4 of the sugar mixture onto each buttered rectangle. Sprinkle about 1/4 cup drained raisins over each rectangle and roll tightly starting from the narrowest side to make a fat roll. Seal edges by pinching with fingers and cut into 3/4-inch thick slices with a sharp knife or a piece of thread. Place slices on well-buttered baking sheets and then lightly press the rolls down and out. Cover and let rise in a warm place about 1 hour. Bake in a preheated 375° oven about 15 minutes, until lightly browned. Cool on racks.

Make an icing by combining confectioners' sugar with cream and the Rum used for soaking the raisins. Add more Rum or cream to taste. Drizzle over buns while still warm.

Makes about 2 dozen buns

Note: The "rummy" raisins can be heated with the milk and added to the dough itself if you prefer.

Rum

RUM CAKE
Baked in a tube pan and not frosted,
this cake is rich, moist and "different"

Cake:
2-1/2 cups sifted all-purpose flour
1 teaspoon baking soda
1 teaspoon baking powder
1/4 teaspoon salt
1/2 cup chopped walnuts
1/2 cup chopped dates
1/3 cup halved maraschino cherries
 (8-ounce bottle)
1/2 pound butter
1 cup granulated sugar
2 eggs
grated peel from 1 large orange
1-1/4 cups sour milk or buttermilk

Syrup:
1 cup granulated sugar
reserved cherry juice
juice of 1 large orange
1 cup light Rum

Cake: Preheat oven to 350°. Butter well and lightly flour an angel food or bundt cake pan. Sift together into a bowl the flour, baking soda, baking powder and salt. Lightly stir in walnuts, dates and well-drained cherries (reserve cherry juice for syrup). Cream butter and sugar together, beat in eggs and orange rind. Add flour mixture alternately with sour milk or buttermilk, stirring just to combine. Pour into prepared tube pan. Bake 1 hour or until a toothpick inserted in center comes out clean. Do not remove from pan.

Syrup: Dissolve sugar in cherry juice and stir in Rum. Pour over the cake while it is still warm (this may take several applications as the syrup seeps slowly into the cake). Leave in pan overnight or until served.

Serves 12 to 16

RUM CARAMEL SAUCE
Very thick, rich and caloric

1-1/4 cups granulated sugar
1/8 teaspoon salt
1/2 cup heavy cream, warmed
1/2 teaspoon light Rum
1/2 teaspoon vanilla extract

Melt sugar and salt in a heavy pan over low heat, stirring to prevent burning. Remove pan from heat and slowly stir in warmed cream, Rum and vanilla; stir together until smooth. Keep warm over hot water until serving time. Use as a dessert fondue with slices of apple, pear, banana; serve with ice cream or use as a topping on angel food or sponge cake, sprinkled with toasted almonds.

POPPY SEED RUM CAKE
Light and lovely with a crunchy texture

3/4 cup poppy seeds
3/4 cup milk
3/4 cup butter or margarine
1-1/2 cups granulated sugar
1 tablespoon dark Rum
2 cups sifted all-purpose flour
2 teaspoons baking powder
4 egg whites, stiffly beaten
Rum Filling, following
Chocolate Icing, page 80

Soak poppy seeds in milk 5 hours or overnight. Cream butter and gradually add sugar; beat in poppy seeds with milk and Rum. Sift flour with baking powder and gradually add to creamed mixture. Fold in beaten egg whites and spread in 2 buttered 9-inch layer-cake pans. Bake in preheated 375° oven for 20 minutes or until it tests done. Cool slightly in pan and then turn out onto racks. When completely cool, spread one layer with Rum Filling. Top with other layer and ice with Chocolate Icing.

RUM FILLING
Rich and luscious with chopped nuts

4 egg yolks
2 cups milk
3 tablespoons cornstarch
1 cup granulated sugar
1/4 teaspoon salt
2 tablespoons dark Rum
1 cup chopped walnuts or pecans

In a saucepan combine egg yolks with 1/2 cup of the milk. Mix together cornstarch, sugar and salt and add to the egg mixture. Stir in remaining milk and Rum. Bring to a boil over low heat, stirring constantly. Cook 5 minutes. Cool. Stir in nuts and spread between cooled cake layers.

Rum

CHRISTMAS FRUIT MINCE
Great for pies, tarts or turnovers

2 pounds green cooking apples, peeled and
   chopped
1 pound carrots, ground
1/2 pound beef suet, ground
1 pound raisins, ground
1 pound sultanas (golden raisins), ground
1/2 pound currants
1/4 pound mixed candied peel, chopped
   (homemade, page 76, or purchased)
juice and ground rind of 1 lemon
1-1/2 teaspoons ground nutmeg
1/2 teaspoon each ground cloves, ground
   cinnamon, ground allspice and salt
1/4 cup dark Rum and 1/4 cup light Rum
   (or 1/2 cup dark Rum)
1 pound (2-1/4 cups) granulated sugar

Combine ingredients and let stand approximately
24 hours at room temperature. Pack in jars or
plastic containers and store in the refrigerator for
at least a month or up to a year. Use this delicious
filling for pie or tart shells (see Basics) or for
turnovers. Serve hot or cold with Apricot Hard
Sauce, page 58.
Makes 3 quarts or more

PUMPKIN RUM CAKE
Bright orange layers with a maple-Rum flavor

1/4 pound butter or margarine
1 cup granulated sugar
1 cup packed light brown sugar
2 eggs
1 cup cooked, mashed pumpkin
3 cups sifted cake flour
4 teaspoons baking soda
1/2 teaspoon salt
1/2 cup light Rum
1/2 cup chopped walnuts or pecans (optional)
2 teaspoons maple syrup or 1 teaspoon
   maple extract
Bourbon Puff, page 129

Preheat oven to 350°. Grease and lightly flour two
9-inch or three 8-inch layer-cake pans. Cream butter and slowly add sugars, beating until light and
fluffy. Beat in eggs and pumpkin. Sift dry ingredients together 3 times and add to creamed mixture
alternately with Rum, beginning and ending with
flour mixture. Fold nuts and maple syrup into
mixture. Divide batter evenly into cake pans and
bake 30 minutes or until cake tests done. Cool. Fill
and frost with Bourbon Puff.
Serves 12 or more

PRALINE PUMPKIN-RUM PIE
A delicate fluffy filling with
crunchy praline under and over

pastry for a single-crust pie, see Basics
1/4 cup light Rum
1/4 cup cold water
1 envelope unflavored gelatin
3/4 cup packed light brown sugar
1 1-pound can cooked pumpkin (2 cups)
3 tablespoons milk
1 teaspoon or more ginger-flavored Brandy
1 teaspoon ground cinnamon
1/2 teaspoon ground nutmeg
1-1/4 teaspoons salt
1 cup heavy cream, whipped
Praline Crunch, following
additional whipped cream for garnish

Preheat oven to 425°. Prepare 1 recipe Basic Pastry and use 1/4 of dough for shell; refrigerate or freeze remainder. Roll out dough as directed in recipe and line a 9-inch pie pan. Pierce shell with tines of fork and bake for 10 to 12 minutes. Cool.

Combine Rum and water in a saucepan and sprinkle gelatin over. Place over low heat; stir constantly until gelatin dissolves, 2 or 3 minutes. Remove from heat and add brown sugar; stir until dissolved. In a bowl combine pumpkin, milk, Brandy, cinnamon, nutmeg and salt. Gradually blend in gelatin mixture; stir until smooth. Fold in whipped cream. Sprinkle 1 cup Praline Crunch over bottom of baked pastry shell. Turn pumpkin mixture into shell. Chill until firm. At serving time garnish with whipped cream and remaining Crunch. Serves 8 to 10

PRALINE CRUNCH
Also delicious on ice cream or pudding

4 tablespoons butter
1/2 cup granulated sugar
1 cup coarsely chopped pecans

Melt butter in a small skillet. Stir in sugar and pecan meats. Cook over moderate heat, stirring constantly, until sugar mixture begins to turn golden, about 3 minutes. Remove from heat and spread onto buttered foil or a smooth buttered surface. Cool. Crumble into pieces.
Makes a very generous amount for 1 pie, can be stretched for 2

Rum

RUM-LIME PIE
Soft, cloud-like meringue cradles Rum-lime filling

Meringue Shell:
3 egg whites (room temperature)
1/4 teaspoon cream of tartar
3/4 cup granulated sugar

Filling:
3 egg yolks
1/3 cup granulated sugar
1/4 cup fresh lime juice
2 tablespoons dark Rum
1 teaspoon grated lime rind
green food coloring
1-1/2 cups heavy cream

Meringue Shell: Preheat oven to 275°. Beat the 3 egg whites until foamy, sprinkle with cream of tartar and continue to beat until they stand in peaks. Gradually add sugar, beating until stiff. Spread in well-buttered pie pan and bake 20 minutes, then raise oven temperature to 300° and bake 40 minutes longer. Cool on rack.
Filling: While meringue is baking, make the filling. In a heavy saucepan combine egg yolks, sugar, lime juice and Rum. Cook, stirring constantly, over a low heat until thickened but not firm. Stir in lime rind and cool. Add a few drops of food coloring (don't be alarmed at the bright yellow-green color). Whip 1 cup of the cream and fold into the cooled filling (which now turns an appetizing pale green). Turn the filling into the meringue shell and chill for 24 hours. Just before serving whip the remaining 1/2 cup of cream, sweeten and lightly flavor with Rum; top each serving with a dollop.
Serves 6 to 8

RUM TRUFFLES

Golden Rum and Crème de Cacao combine with cashews to flavor these elegant candies

2-1/4 cups packed light brown sugar
3/4 cup water
3/4 cup medium Rum
2 cups salted cashews
7 squares baking chocolate
4 tablespoons butter, sweet or lightly salted
1/4 cup light corn syrup
1 tablespoon Crème de Cacao
1/2 cup sifted unsweetened cocoa powder
1/2 cup sifted confectioners' sugar
1/4 teaspoon ground cinnamon

Butter sides of a 1-quart saucepan and measure in the first 3 ingredients. Stir constantly until a full boil is reached; then continue to cook uncovered over high heat stirring occasionally until the mixture reaches the hard crack stage (about 295°). While it is cooking, spread the cashews on a buttered baking sheet. Pour the hot syrup over the nuts. When the praline is cold and hard, break it into small pieces and grind to a powder in the blender. Strain to remove any unpowdered bits.

In the top of a double boiler melt the chocolate and butter with the corn syrup and Crème de Cacao. Remove from the heat and gradually work in the praline powder (you will need to use your hands near the end). Shape the mixture into uneven balls about the size of a giant olive or small truffle. Sift together cocoa, confectioners' sugar and cinnamon into a shallow bowl. Roll the candies in the cocoa mixture; chill until hard. Store in an airtight container.
Makes about 50

MANGO RUM TARTS

An exotic touch of the tropics

Pastry for Tart Shells, see Basics
2 large mangoes, peeled
1/2 cup granulated sugar
1/4 cup medium or dark Rum
1 teaspoon cornstarch
1 teaspoon lemon or lime juice
1 egg yolk
1/4 teaspoon ground ginger
sweetened Rum-flavored whipped cream

Prepare pastry as directed; set aside 1/2 of dough for shells and refrigerate or freeze remainder. Press dough into 6 to 8 tart shells, pierce with tines of fork and bake at 425° for 10 to 12 minutes. Cool.

Thinly slice mangoes into saucepan; add sugar and Rum. Cook over low heat for 10 minutes, stirring occasionally. Combine cornstarch with lemon or lime juice and stir into egg yolk. Add a little of the hot fruit to egg mixture and then stir egg mixture into kettle. Continue to cook over low heat, stirring constantly, until thick and smooth. Stir in ginger. Cool and pour into baked tart shells. Serve with sweetened, Rum-flavored whipped cream.
Makes 6 to 8 tarts

Vodka, Gin, Sake and Tequila

VODKA AND GIN

Vodka is a spirit generally made from grain but left unflavored. It can be made from potatoes, dates or any source of carbohydrate. It has relatively little flavor, little or no aroma, and is of little value in cooking. It is an excellent base, however, for making your own liqueurs and the very high-proof Vodkas are suitable for flambéing.

    Gin, however, is usually based upon denatured alcohol and is flavored with juniper berries and often with additional berries, roots or barks of plants. Its aroma and flavor can be excellent additions to pork dishes, sauerkraut and strangely enough, potato salad. Use Gin where vinegar would be your first thought.

SAKE AND TEQUILA

Sake is made from rice which is cleansed and steamed and then allowed to ferment. When the fermentation is nearly over more rice is added. The sake is drawn off, filtered and put into casks for maturing. It is colorless and rather sweet, with a bitter aftertaste that the Japanese and Okinawans particularly enjoy.

As rice has little flavor Sake can't be expected to have much either. However there are more than a dozen different types of Sake and they can be roughly categorized as *mirin* (for cooking), *toso* (sweet and spicy—reserved for drinking on special occasions) and *seishu* (commonly drunk with food).

When cold, the flavor is somewhat yeasty, though the Okinawan Sake, which is somewhat rougher than the Japanese Sake, is traditionally enjoyed cold. Most of us prefer the drink served warm and there is a carry-over into cooking. Sake seems to enhance food flavors best when both the food and the Sake are warm. If you have Sake on hand which you don't care to drink, use it in marinades (as you would wine) or in preparing Japanese dishes.

Tequila is distilled from the fermented juices of the Mexican century-plant cactus. White Tequila is unaged and distilled at about 100° proof. Gold Tequila has been aged in oak vats for at least four years, has more flavor and is kinder to the tongue.

No one can say Tequila is tasteless! It's as prickly on the palate as the cactus it comes from. The fiery dryness can be an interesting addition to spicy foods. When experimenting with the spirit, try it first in highly seasoned Mexican dishes. *Gávilan Tequila Liqueur* is a sweetened Tequila which can be interesting with tropical fruits. *Pulque* is also made from the milky juice of the cactus. It is fermented but not distilled and is usually drunk when freshly made . . . which means you don't find it widely distributed outside of Mexico. No loss, most people feel!

Vodka, Gin, Sake and Tequila

MEXICAN SHRIMP
The acid in the lime actually "cooks" the shrimp, making their texture firm and white

1 pound raw or cooked shrimp, shelled
   and deveined
1/2 cup light olive oil
1 garlic clove
juice of 2 limes
dash cayenne
3 hot green chili peppers, chopped
3 scallions, chopped
2 tablespoons Tequila
Tabasco to taste

Combine ingredients and marinate 2 hours if shrimp have been precooked, 6 hours for raw shrimp.
Serves 4 or more as an appetizer

POTATO SALAD WITH GIN
Not only different but delicious

8 new potatoes
1/4 cup Gin
1/4 cup light olive oil
4 scallions or 2 large shallots, chopped
freshly ground pepper
2 tablespoons chopped fresh parsley
1 tablespoon coarse salt

Wash and cook potatoes; peel while still hot. Slice 1/4 inch thick and arrange a layer in a salad bowl. Sprinkle with Gin, olive oil, scallions or shallots and pepper. Repeat layering. Just before serving toss with parsley and salt. Good hot or cold.
Serves 4

MEXICAN COLD SOUP
Tequila and lime juice add
south-of-the-border flavor

1-1/4 cups beef consommé
2 cups tomato juice
1 tablespoon finely chopped scallions
1 tablespoon finely chopped green pepper
3 tablespoons Tequila
juice of 1/2 lime
1/2 teaspoon salt

Combine ingredients and chill. Serve icy cold with any kind of corn chips, salt sticks or cubes of cheese.
Makes 6 appetizer portions

JELLIED CUCUMBER GIN SOUP
Juniper juice gives it a little nip

1 envelope (1 tablespoon) unflavored gelatin
2 cups chicken stock
1 small onion, minced
1/4 teaspoon salt
1 teaspoon chopped fresh dill, or 1/4 teaspoon
　　dill weed
2 tablespoons lemon juice
1/4 teaspoon Worcestershire sauce
dash Tabasco
freshly ground pepper
3 tablespoons Gin
2 medium cucumbers
3 tablespoons chopped pimiento
2 tablespoons finely chopped parsley
lemon slices for garnish

Soften gelatin in 1 cup of the chicken stock. Simmer remaining broth with onion, salt and dill for 10 minutes. Remove from heat. Stir in softened gelatin, lemon juice, Worcestershire sauce, Tabasco and pepper. Stir until gelatin is thoroughly dissolved; add Gin. Cool and chill until soup is syrupy. Peel, seed and coarsely grate cucumbers (by hand or with blender). Stir cucumbers, pimiento and parsley into jellied broth. Refrigerate at least 4 hours. Garnish with a twisted lemon slice. Serves 6

SZEKELY GULYAS
Transylvanian pork goulash

1 medium onion, chopped
1 clove garlic, chopped or pressed
2 slices bacon (or about 1 tablespoon bacon fat)
1 pound pork shoulder, cut in 1-inch pieces
1 tablespoon paprika
1 teaspoon granulated sugar
1/2 teaspoon salt
1/2 teaspoon caraway seeds
1/4 teaspoon coarsely cracked pepper
1-2/3 cups chicken stock
2 cups chopped tomatoes, or 1 16-ounce can
　　tomatoes
1 cup dry white wine
1 16-ounce can sauerkraut
2 tablespoons Gin
1/2 cup sour cream

Sauté onion, garlic and bacon or bacon fat. Remove the vegetables and brown pork in the fat. Sprinkle with paprika, sugar, salt, caraway seeds and pepper. Stir in chicken stock, tomatoes, white wine and sauerkraut. Simmer 1-1/2 hours. Check now and then during cooking; if goulash seems dry add 1/2 cup water. Stir in Gin and sour cream just before serving (do not bring to a boil again). Stew can be reheated even with the sour cream in it. Serves 3 to 4

Vodka, Gin, Sake and Tequila

AVOCADO QUICHE
A Mexican beauty

Crust:
pastry for single-crust pie, see Basics
1 tablespoon poppy seeds
1 tablespoon soft butter

Filling:
1 cup grated Swiss cheese (1/4 pound)
1 avocado
4 eggs
1 teaspoon salt
1/4 teaspoon coarsely ground pepper
pinch sugar
1 tablespoon Tequila
1 tablespoon lime juice
1/4 teaspoon Tabasco
1 cup heavy cream
3 to 4 bacon slices, cut in half

Crust: Prepare 1 recipe Basic Pastry; set aside 1/4 of dough (about 1 cup) for pie shell and refrigerate or freeze remainder. Gently stir poppy seeds into dough with a fork. Roll out on lightly floured board and use to line a 9-inch pie pan. Spread with soft butter.
Filling: Sprinkle grated cheese over the crust. Mash avocado and blend with eggs, salt, pepper, sugar, Tequila, lime juice and Tabasco; add heavy cream. Pour over cheese and bake 15 minutes. Reduce temperature to 300° and bake 40 minutes longer. Garnish with bacon which has been cooked and rolled, placing a roll made of 1/2 strip of bacon on each portion for garnish.
Serves 6 to 8

CRAB MEAT STUFFING
FOR TURKEY OR FISH
Increase the bread and decrease the crab if
the pocketbook complains

1/4 cup chopped shallots
2 cups sliced mushrooms
4 tablespoons butter or margarine
12 ounces (3 cups) crab meat
   (fresh, canned or frozen)
1 teaspoon salt
1/2 teaspoon poultry seasoning
4 teaspoons fresh dill, chopped
1/4 cup chopped parsley
1/4 cup Gin or dry Vermouth, or some of both
4 cups torn bread

Sauté shallots and mushrooms (this is a good place to use mushroom stems) in butter. Add crab, seasonings and spirits; stir in bread. Use as stuffing for turkey or fish.
Makes about 8 cups of stuffing

Glossary and Indexes

Glossary

Alcohol A colorless, volatile, flammable liquid.

Cordial See *Liqueur.*

Crème or *Cream* A sweetened spirit or liqueur. Crèmes are used chiefly in flavoring desserts or with vegetables which are naturally sweet, though many culinary uses are possible.

Distillation The process of reducing the water content of alcoholic liquids. The alcohol is vaporized by heating the liquid; the gases are then condensed by cooling, forming a more concentrated alcoholic liquid.

Eau de Vie See *Fruit Brandy.*

Fruit Brandy A liqueur made by mashing fruit, allowing the pulp to ferment and then distilling it. Sugar is seldom added. Also called white alcohol or eau de vie (water of life), a fruit Brandy is very dry, clear and colorless. The flavor is concentrated and the bouquet marked, making these liqueurs excellent in cooking. However, as they are distilled from thousands of raspberries, strawberries, plums or whatever the fruit may be, they are expensive.

Fruit-flavored Brandy A liqueur based upon Brandy made from grapes but flavored with the fruit named on the label. Generally they are sweetened but not as heavily as crèmes. Fruit-flavored Brandies are the least expensive source of any given fruit flavor (other than making your own liqueur).

Grain Neutral Spirits A spirit distilled from the fermented mash of grain at or above 190° proof and bottled at not less than 80° proof. An inexpensive base for homemade liqueurs.

Liqueur or *Cordial* All perfumed or flavored drinkable spirits sweetened by the addition of sugar.

Proof A measure of the percent of alcohol by volume. The word comes from the early days when sailors aboard British Men-O-War received a daily ration of heavy Jamaican Rum. Each day the grog barrel was "proofed" before the rations were handed round. Equal quantities of the spirit and gunpowder were mixed and burned. If it burned evenly with a blue flame, it was said to have been proved and the quartermaster was reconfirmed as an honest man who didn't water the grog down for his own gain.

Each degree of proof is equal to one-half of one percent of alcohol. Thus a bottle labeled 90° proof is 45 percent alcohol. For cooking, the less alcohol (the lower the degree of proof) the better, as alcohol evaporates with heat but flavors remain. The exception, of course, is flambéing, where a high proof is necessary to produce a good flame.

Spirit Any drinkable alcoholic liquid obtained through distillation.

White Alcohol. See *Fruit Brandy.*

Index of Spirits by Label

The page references in this index refer only to specific mentions of the liqueur listed. Once you have determined the basic flavor of a liqueur as explained in the text, check the chapter recipes for references to that flavor. For example, if a recipe calls for orange-flavored liqueur, Cointreau, Triple Sec or Grand Marnier may be used.

Index of Spirits by Label

Recipe Index

Recipe Index

Biographical Notes

BEVERLY ANDERSON BARBOUR

Beverly Barbour's career as a nutrition consultant and food writer has spanned six continents and brought her into contact with almost every major cuisine of the world. But her work started on a much less exotic level in her native North Dakota, where she taught the women and children of an Indian reservation the importance of good diet. Later she became Director of Home Economics for the Wheat Flour Institute in Chicago and then went to Asia to teach nutrition to the peoples of Japan, Korea, Taiwan and the Philippines. Food consulting assignments have also taken her to a number of countries in Latin America and Europe, to two African nations and to Pakistan. On writing assignments for magazines she has studied the foods and reviewed the restaurants of such diverse places as Indonesia, Thailand, Australia, Afghanistan and Ecuador.

Mrs. Barbour's syndicated food column "Bev's Bits and Bites" has served as the basis for five prior cookbooks. She also is food editor of *Club Management Magazine,* restaurant reviewer for *Nation's Restaurant News,* conducts a series of semi-weekly radio interviews with chefs and serves as diet and nutrition consultant for the American Bakers Association.

Recently she was hostess for ten half-hour television programs called "Cooking by Countries" for NBC, authored a special supplement on wine and spirits for *The New York Times* and contributed a series on "Cooking with Spirits" to *Vintage Magazine.* A dame de la Chaine and member of the Wine and Food Society, Beverly currently lives and works in Hyde Park, New York, where her husband, Henry Ogden Barbour, is president of the Culinary Institute of America.

DAVID YEADON

Though a city planner by profession, David Yeadon's wanderlust and robust interest in food and wine constantly draw him to remote corners of Europe and North America, sampling and chronicling the gastronomic offerings as writer, artist and photographer. Born in England, he has been a restaurant critic in Tehran and, since 1970, while living in the United States, has written and/or illustrated 14 books, mostly concerned with food and travel. These include a number of guides to California and New England, a cookbook, *Sumptuous Indulgence on a Shoestring,* and *The New York Book of Bars, Pubs and Taverns.* He presently lives in New York City.